MW00775556

DETERRENCE

DETERRENCE

LAWRENCE FREEDMAN

polity

Copyright © Lawrence Freedman 2004

The right of Lawrence Freedman to be identified as Author of this Work has been asserted in accordance with the UK Copyright, Designs and Patents Act 1988.

First published in 2004 by Polity Press

Polity Press
65 Bridge Street
Cambridge CB2 1UR, UK

Polity Press
350 Main Street
Malden, MA 02148, USA

All rights reserved. Except for the quotation of short passages for the purposes of criticism and review, no part of this publication may be reproduced, stored in a retrieval system, or transmitted, in any form or by any means, electronic, mechanical, photocopying, recording or otherwise, without the prior permission of the publisher.

ISBN: 0-7456-3112-6
ISBN: 0-7456-3113-4 (pb)

A catalogue record for this book is available from the British Library and has been applied for from the Library of Congress.

Typeset in 11 on 13 pt Berling
by SNP Best-set Typesetter Ltd., Hong Kong
Printed and bound in the United Kingdom by MPG Books, Bodmin, Cornwall

For further information on Polity, visit our website:
www.polity.co.uk

CONTENTS

vi   Contents

ACKNOWLEDGEMENTS

Thanks are due to Rachel Kerr who as editor at Polity first persuaded me to write this and when I had agreed made sure that I did so. She is now happily my colleague at King's College. Like all students of international relations in general and deterrence in particular, I am indebted to Robert Jervis and Patrick Morgan and I am very greateful for their comments on an earlier version of this manuscript. This version has also benefited greatly from comments by Colin Gray, Beatrice Heuser and Lucia Zedner.

This is an original book but it has its genesis in a paper written in 1996, *Does Deterrence Have a Future?*, Future Roles Series Papers No. 5, for the Sandia national laboratories, New Mexico. The issues are also explored more historically and less theoretically in my *Evolution of Nuclear Strategy*, 3rd edition, London: Palgrave, 2003. Some of the material in chapter 6 appeared in *The Washington Quarterly* (spring 2003) as 'Prevention, not Pre-emption'.

INTRODUCTION

Throughout the cold war the concept of deterrence was central to all strategic discourse. Every strategic move of the West was made with reference to its requirements, and eventually this was also the case with the Soviet bloc. This special status as policy transferred into respectful treatment as a concept, reflected in libraries of books and numerous articles. As is often the case with orthodoxies, deterrence began to attract the mockery and disgust of the disaffected and hostile. Then, abruptly, with the end of the cold war, it was no longer orthodox. The concept appeared overextended and vulnerable to the criticisms of politicians and academics, and then to the loss of the adversary that had served as its focal point. In a more complex international environment deterrence seemed redundant as a policy while, as the result of the sustained critique, more suspect as a concept. From dominating Western strategic thinking it moved to the margins. Friends slipped away. The first to go were the doves, uneasy about a policy reliant on threats rather than inducements, and stressing military issues above the political and economic. Later some regretted their desertion, for eventually the anti-deterrence theme was taken up as part of a more hawkish determination to take the initiative. The hawks were not looking for a soft option but rather for an escape from deterrence's presumption of restraint and tendency to passivity.

During the course of 2002 President George W. Bush set in motion what appeared to be a radical shift in US security policy, from deterrence to pre-emption. Reliance on deterrence assumed that the threat of force could contain the hostile behaviour of others. A move to pre-emption, which also has a long, though less distinguished, history betrayed a loss of confidence. There were some threats that could not be deterred and must be dealt with before they could be realized. This shift was prompted by the terrorist attack on the United States of 11 September 2001, an event so traumatic in its impact that a reference to '9/11' is normally sufficient in itself to infer a turning point in international affairs. After 9/11 the Bush Administration decided that Saddam Hussein's regime in Iraq was so lawless and vicious and so committed to its arsenal of weapons of mass destruction that unless it was dealt with in short order it could make possible an even deadlier terrorist attack on the United States, on its forces abroad or its allies.

In March 2003 American, supported by British and, to a lesser extent, Australian forces mounted an invasion of Iraq and within a few weeks the country was under effective coalition occupation. It soon became evident, however, that the threat from weapons of mass destruction had not been quite so imminent as had been alleged pre-war, suggesting that it had been as deterrable as the war's critics had insisted. At the same time the downfall of a particularly oppressive regime was met with general rejoicing and this, in itself, could be taken to justify the war's successful prosecution, qualified by evident problems in restoring security and basic services, and in embarking on reconstruction after decades of misrule, wars and sanctions.

The war also raised questions about American power. It appeared unstoppable. The Bush Administration had brushed aside dissent in the United Nations, leaving all the other major powers on the Security Council other than Britain – France, Germany, Russia and China – objecting but effectively impotent. Such military resistance as the Iraqi regime could muster was swept away with ease. The sort of heavy casualty attacks that might have made the coalition forces stop in their tracks, from weapons of mass destruction or international terrorism, failed to materialize. In the early 1990s American military planners had begun to talk about 'full spectrum dominance' in military operations and now that is what seemed to have been achieved. With military expenditure set at a level equivalent to the rest of the world combined, there were no obvious limits on how this could be used. The only obvious counter left was nuclear strength. Other than that, if the USA was to be deterred, it was less likely to be because of some balancing military capability than because of the costs and frustrations associated with running territories, such as Afghanistan and Iraq, for which it had acquired some responsibility.

All this meant that running parallel to the American debate about how to use this power to deal with threats still lurking in the international environment was a debate else-where about how to cope with American power. The issue was not new. It had been at the back of every big crisis since the end of the cold war. Is the United States, as the lone superpower, bound to assert its dominant position, insisting that its interests must take precedence over all others and casting aside international organizations when they fail to do so? Or can this power be harnessed and channelled for the international good, not only respecting the rights of other countries but also listening hard to what they have to say? The controversy over Iraq pushed the debate in one direc-tion because the Americans appeared hyper-active, charged by their critics as being on the rampage, fired up by dreams of world domination and guided by doctrines of pre-emption. Under President Bill Clinton, however, the debate had gone in another direction, with an appearance more of lethargy. For much of the 1990s, especially following the debacle in Somalia, the overall impression was that the USA was going to be a most reluctant intervener. There is there-fore a contemporary concern not only about the specifics of US foreign policy, but also about a situation in which the shifts and turns of US foreign policy matter as much as they do. Yet pre-emption is of limited benefit as a guide to what form US security policy *should* take in the future and what form it is likely to take. The condition of 'imminence', supposedly the critical factor determining whether pre-emption is warranted, has to be stretched to its limits, and even then the cases where this will appear as a wise and useful policy will be few and far between. Moreover, the ambiguity about situations in which it might be justified means that elevating this notion to a security doctrine rather than an occasional stratagem by the USA creates opportunities for states that might use new-fangled notions of pre-emption as rationalization when embarking on old-fashioned aggression.

Does that mean that deterrence, so explicitly discarded in policy towards Iraq, might still have a role to play? To answer this question, the first part of this book unpacks the concept. I do not attempt to offer a full treatment of all the theoretical and policy issues surrounding deterrence. There are well covered in a recent book by Patrick Morgan.[1] My aim, which is taken forward in the second part of the book, is to develop a particular framework for thinking about deterrence. The starting point is that deterrence does not offer a self-contained strategic relationship but is part of a wider set of relationships. The degree to which a deterrence relationship was institutionalized during the cold war was therefore misleading and anomalous. Conditional threats are a regular form of communication, but usually in concert with other forms, and it is their combined impact over time that must be assessed. On this basis I argue for a *norms-based* as much as an *interests-based* approach. An interests-based approach remains straightforward. Those who contemplate harming certain well-defined interests should know the consequences. A norms-based approach requires reinforcing certain values to the point where it is well understood that they must not be violated. This involves deterrence, in that part of this exercise may be punishing or threatening to punish violations, although the process of establishing norms takes in all elements of foreign policy.

The attraction of a norms-based approach is that it may better reflect how deterrence actually works in practice, through actors internalizing a sense of the appropriate limits on their actions. The utilitarian approach, out of which the original concept of deterrence originated, has been qualified over time by an awareness of the importance of emotions and values. Not surprisingly, deterrence works best when the targets are able to act rationally, and when the deterrer and the deterred are working within a sufficiently shared normative framework so that it is possible to inculcate a sense of appropriate behaviour in defined situations that can be reinforced by a combination of social pressures and a sense of fair and effective punishment. Norms, therefore, do not develop and exist independently of assertions of power and interest. Indeed, to start with they are likely to be a close reflection of the predominant interests within a power structure, but once they have taken hold they may not always follow exactly the shifts and turns of political fortune and fashion, and may even acquire a subversive quality. One can say the same for concepts. The language we use to identify our interests, give meaning to our power and explain our actions is infused with conventional wisdom and uncomfortable rationalizations, moral presumptions and embedded axioms. The conceptual frameworks adopted by policy-makers are likely to be as eclectic, inchoate and self-contradictory as they are systematic and rigorous, but that does not mean that they can be readily dismissed. One task for academics working in policy areas is to engage with these frameworks and in so doing help explore their impact on how foreign policy problems come to be structured and possible solutions assessed. The biography of the concept of deterrence is in itself one of the most remarkable demonstrations of the interaction between an apparently abstract conceptual discourse and some of the most challenging issues of military strategy and practical politics.

1 THE RISE AND FALL OF DETERRENCE

Origins

Manipulating another's behaviour through threats is a natural phenomenon. The fittest often survive through persuading potential predators that they are too fast to be caught, that they will fight back if they are, and that even if they can be overwhelmed, they are inedible. Some of these forms of natural deterrence can be quite subtle, and even rely on confusing opponents. The owl eyes on the wings of the Caligo butterfly serve to persuade birds to keep their distance. Monarch butterflies have to make some sacrifices to sustain deterrence because bluejays only learn not to eat them after their first attempt makes them sick. When one jumping spider approaches another, leg-waving behaviour is used to mark out territory. There is a fly that has acquired wing markings that resemble the legs of the jumping spider, and an ability to create the impression of leg-waving sufficient to persuade a potentially predatory spider that it is in the presence of another so that it backs away.[1] These examples indicate that deterrence can be instinctive and still be based on bluff, but for the purposes of this book deterrence is concerned with deliberate attempts to manipulate the behaviour of others through conditional threats.

The first such attempt, if the Bible is taken literally, followed the creation. The first words used, spoken by God to man, contain a deterrent threat. To his opening promise – 'you may eat from any fruit in the garden' – was added a critical exception. If you eat the fruit of the 'Tree of Conscience', God warned Adam, 'you will be doomed to die'. This first deterrent threat was followed by the first deterrence failure, as Eve tasted the forbidden fruit and persuaded Adam to do the same, and then by an example of lax enforcement, as the pair were banished from Eden but allowed a much delayed death. The rest of the Bible is concerned with God's attempt to regain authority over the beings he had created. Clerics have for centuries used the promise of heaven and the threat of hell to remind believers of the need to conduct their earthly lives with a view to how they might be rewarded or punished for eternity in the next.

The idea that demonstrations of military strength might lead adversaries to restrain themselves was reflected in the Roman motto of *Si vis pacem, para bellum* (if you wish for peace, prepare for war). This has always been the standard argument for maintaining a war-like appearance even while denying war-like intentions. Yet the word 'deterrence', at least in its origins, goes beyond encouraging prudent calculations in others. Its etymology starts with the Latin *deterre* – to frighten from or away. English usage developed reasonably consistently in references, from the caution that results from an appreciation of possible hazards in almost any setting to attempts to induce caution by threats of pain. There is thus an instrumental sense to the concept: to scare off another with a purpose. Can the act of scaring another be dispassionate and cold-blooded? This is what strategic deterrence appears to require.

The confidence that another's calculations might be readily manipulated to prevent them doing harm looms large in the thinking of the utilitarian philosopher Jeremy Bentham, whose ideas developed during the late eighteenth century. He attacked the notion that punishments should be ad hoc, arguing instead that a deterrent effect could be

developed if there was both a degree of clarity and pre-
dictability in sentencing along with proportionality between
the crime and the punishment. As a utilitarian he supposed
that criminals, along with everybody else, were rational and
self-interested, and could calculate when the costs of punishment would outweigh the potential benefits of crime.

Bentham used a term that was common at the time, but
which has now passed out of use: determent. This is defined
by the *Oxford English Dictionary* as being 'The action or fact
of deterring, a means of deterring; a deterring circumstance'.
According to Bentham:

> In so far as by the act of punishment exercised on the
> delinquent, other persons at large are considered as deterred
> from the commission of acts of the like obnoxious descrip-
> tion, and the act of punishment is in consequence considered
> as endued with the quality of DETERMENT. It is by the
> impression made on the will of those persons, an impression
> made in this case not by the act itself, but by the idea of it,
> accompanied with the eventual expectation of a similar
> EVIL, as about to be eventually produced in their own
> instances, that the ultimately intentional result is considered
> as produced: and in this case it is also said to be produced by
> the EXAMPLE, or by the force of EXAMPLE.[2]

Determent remains a potentially useful word for it describes
a situation in which what was intended has been achieved.
Over time, however, it has been replaced by the word that
describes the strategy intended to produce the effect: deterrence. By the end of the nineteenth century the term 'deterrence' was being used to refer to the policy of influencing
the behaviour of potential wrongdoers through the prospect
of punishment.

The criminological model is often employed, not only in
terms of needing to prevent aggressive actions outside of
international law, but also in terms of a direct analogy with
the domestic system of criminal justice. In the first authoritative presentation of the doctrine of deterrence by the US
Government in 1954, Secretary of State John Foster Dulles,

a lawyer who was inclined to see all aspects of foreign policy as branches of criminal law, set out the analogy:

> We keep locks on our doors; but we do not have an armed guard in every home. We rely principally on a community security system so well equipped to punish any who break in and steal that, in fact, would-be-aggressors are generally deterred. That is the way of getting maximum protection at bearable cost.[3]

The analogy was of dubious relevance. The obvious difference between security in the domestic and international spheres is that the international lacks a supreme authority able to make and enforce laws, backed by a monopoly of legitimate violence. More seriously, by this time, with the Soviet Union having tested its own nuclear weapons, a policy of deterrence through punishment was always going to be problematic. The likely offenders would have formidable and equivalent means of counter-punishment. Despite these problems, utilitarianism infuses the analysis of deterrence in strategic studies.

Celebration

Contemporary strategic usage is normally traced back to the early airpower theorists of the 1920s and 1930s who wondered whether the only way to prevent air raids on a massive scale was to demonstrate a capacity to retaliate in kind. The gloomy assumption as put by a British Prime Minister, was that the 'bomber will always get through', unstoppable by any defensive measures, causing immense damage to physical infrastructure and public morale when they did so. This encouraged the view that only the prospect of retaliation in kind – an eye for an eye – could act as any sort of restraint. Although the experience of the Second World War revealed a more complex relationship between offence and defence than the theorists had anticipated, in the post-war world this original formulation seemed to be more pertinent than ever. This was because of nuclear weapons. The more it became evident that there was no way to fight a nuclear war without a high risk of utter catastrophe the more discretion began to triumph over valour, and the more compelling became schemes for avoiding war as a means of deciding disputes, even if the differences were thereby left unresolved. As a result, for four decades deterrence dominated debate about grand strategy on both sides of the Iron Curtain, acquiring all the trappings of an orthodoxy.

The first hypothetical thoughts in Britain and the USA about atomic bombs were framed in deterrent terms, as a necessary counter to a prospective German bomb. The sudden and spectacular introduction of the weapons in August 1945 pushed to the fore the idea that future wars might be prevented through the prospect of the intense destruction made possible by the processes of nuclear fission. At the same time there was no great confidence in this. There had, after all, been two world wars in the course of thirty years, and the experience of the first had been thought to be sufficiently bad to serve as a persuasive argument against a second. The gloomy logic was that the arrival of nuclear weapons simply meant that the next world war would finish off the destructive job the previous two had not quite completed. The early official view, and one shared by the general public and the bulk of those scientists responsible for the bomb's creation, was that the only safe course was to prohibit the future use of nuclear power for military purposes.

The failure of disarmament efforts against the backdrop of the developing cold war obliged governments to consider the implications of living with the bomb in a conflictual world. Support for the view that the prospect was not necessarily as dire as had been at first assumed was found in a group around Bernard Brodie, who had made his name as a naval strategist. They argued that here was a power terrible enough to give even the most reckless and aggressive pause for thought. 'Thus far', Brodie observed in 1946, 'the chief purpose of our military establishment has been to win wars.

From now on its chief purpose must be to avert them.'[4] Interestingly, Brodie used the old-fashioned word 'determent' in his edited book, *The Absolute Weapon,* rather than deterrence. While contemporary deterrence theory is traced back to this book, its actual impact at the time was modest. The idea really took root during the early 1950s as the weapons themselves became more plentiful and moved to even more awesome levels of destructive power with the invention of thermonuclear (fusion/hydrogen) weapons, each capable of turning whole cities into rubble. Initially, the USA enjoyed an impressive superiority in nuclear capabilities. At this stage deterrence displayed, at least for the short term, a rough and ready credibility. What is striking is how deterrence policy lasted beyond the short term, and in particular survived the development of Soviet long-range missiles and bombers able to reach the continental United States, which, it had been assumed, would remove its credibility.

To understand its durability a number of important presentational features can be noted. First, deterrence sounded robust without being reckless. Forces were not being used to compel a change in the status quo but only to contain an enemy. As the cold war began to grip international affairs during the late 1940s, the doctrine of containment was first adumbrated, committing the United States to work to prevent further westward expansion by the Soviet Union into Europe. Given the balance of power, neither the roll-back nor the appeasement of communism was acceptable. Containment assumed that communism was naturally expansionist and so could only be held through the threat of force and, if necessary, the realization of this threat at those points where it looked as if it might break out of its limits. It seemed to be the only option – and containment as an objective lent itself to deterrence as a method. Deterrence anticipated aggression, and therefore guarded against being caught by surprise, but it could still be presented as essentially reactive.

Second, it was hard to think of a better way to make sense of a nuclear inventory. As Henry Kissinger later observed:

'The nuclear age turned strategy into deterrence, and deterrence into an esoteric intellectual exercise.'[5] Nuclear weapons appeared to be the means by which the costs could be raised high enough to persuade Moscow not to think about aggression without too much exertion on behalf of the allies. The United States did not develop nuclear weapons in order to deter – but rather in order to win the Second World War and then to exploit the strategic advantage gained though the investment. So long as the USA had superiority, the power of these weapons seemed sufficient to stop any aggressor in its tracks. Once the Soviet Union also acquired a nuclear arsenal, then the advantage was lost, but by this time the political situation had stabilized. If a war had been unavoidable, there would have been every reason to find military alternatives to nuclear weapons. The main threat to this standoff was presumed to be one side stealing a march on the other through some development in weapons technology, or else the clever manipulation of the standoff at the higher levels of escalation by taking risks at the lower levels.

During the 1950s Western governments encouraged the view that they were really prepared to contemplate nuclear war in the battle against totalitarian communism, and discouraged too much speculation as to whether this was little more than bluff. They talked up their own recklessness, as evidenced by another of John Foster Dulles's comments, about the need to be ready 'to go to the brink' during a crisis. In fact, by this time they already supposed that Moscow was unlikely to risk total war and was settling down for the 'long haul' of ideological competition and indirect subversion. Neither side seemed likely to push too hard if the result was almost bound to be mutual suicide. So long as the strategy was deterrence, then nuclear weapons seemed appropriate. Actual nuclear use would be a catastrophe, offending strategic logic as well as ethical principles. But the faint possibility of use, precisely because it would be so catastrophic, left a formidable imprint. Throughout the cold war the nuclear overhang reinforced a sense that the main benefit of force lay in what was held in reserve. The military capacity of the West was never to be used to its full extent. The mind-set was one in which it had become too dangerous to prepare to crush enemies with overwhelming force. Military moves should be designed to create a superior bargaining position. So by the 1970s, with all considerations of force in the West, and not just with nuclear weapons, there was 'a predominance of the latent over the manifest, of the oblique over the direct, of the limited over the general'.[6]

The pertinence of this thought bothered strategists throughout the cold war – yet deterrence seemed to work, maybe better in practice than in theory. This was its third presentational feature. The prospect of nuclear war evidently encouraged a welcome caution all round. War was avoided because politicians made the effort to do so, aware of the consequences of failure. If, as it seemed, there was no way of getting out of the nuclear age, then deterrence made the best of a bad job. While it was often difficult to explain exactly how deterrence had worked its magic, and historians could point to some terrifying moments when catastrophe was only just round the corner, the third world war did not happen, and the fact that the superpowers were scared of the prospect of such a war surely had something to do with its failure to materialize. Total war was avoided, if not all war, and this success benefited not only the United States but also its allies, its potential enemies and the world in general.

Exactly where credit should be given for the 'long peace'[7] remains a matter for debate. Michael Howard judged that it was 'beyond doubt that we effectively deterred the Soviet Union from using military force to achieve its political objectives', adding that 'we have become rather expert at deterrence'. At least one eminent political scientist questioned whether nuclear weapons had played any part at all; few cold war historians were prepared to go so far.[8] Given the undoubted existence of deep antagonism between East and West, it seemed grudging not to attribute at least some of the credit for avoiding yet another total war to the dread of global conflagration involving nuclear exchanges and to the policies adopted, at times by both sides, to reinforce this dread by means of deliberate deterrence.

The fourth presentational advantage enjoyed by deterrence was a reflection of institutional inertia. The durability of the cold war, and in particular the ideological divide at its heart, ensured that there was a relatively tight framework within which all questions of foreign policy and force planning were viewed. This was embedded in the major security organizations, confirmed by every NATO communiqué, Pentagon report and foreign minister's speech, and inculcated into generations of officers, diplomats and politicians, so that it became almost beyond reflection. As every increase in, or recasting of, defence provision and peacetime posturing could be rationalized as being designed to persuade others not to start a war, there was little undertaken that could not be described as deterrence.

Overstretch

Within this framework, deterrence became a matter of any possible contributions to the preservation of the status quo. It was seen to be so benign in its effects that its supporters became ever more ambitious on its behalf. What was to be deterred? The answer moved from strategic war to minor provocations; from specific hostile acts to all hostile acts; from hostile acts directed against oneself to those directed against allies, and even the enemy's enemies; from hostile acts that had yet to materialize to those already set in motion. How were these to be deterred? The answer moved from threats of overwhelming force to a prospect of mutual destruction; from disproportionate to proportionate retaliation; from setting definite obstacles to aggression to warnings that should aggression occur the consequences could be beyond calculation. Because it covered allies, deterrence was, from the start, 'extended'; because it covered potential enemies it was 'mutual'. Deterrent threats had been

employed at times of crisis, when they had become 'immediate', and then had a lingering impact of a 'general' nature.
They had been designed to persuade the enemy through
'denial' that gains would be hard to come by, and through
'punishment' that whatever gains might be obtained would
soon be outweighed through the imposition of intolerable
pain.

Too little deterrence courted disaster; too much might
slide into an aggressive posture, at least in the eyes of potential opponents. Attempts to define these higher and lower
points, in relationship to prevailing assessments of the strategic balance, became the main business of the Western policy
community for the duration of the cold war. Quite distinctive and often opposed policies could all be described as
deterrent. The advocates of particular measures would
explain how they conformed to this authoritative idea,
whether or not this claim was a true reflection of its inspi-
ration or had any validity at all.

Once deterrence became doctrine, then it was elevated to
the status of a general theory of strategic relationships, and
was defended and attacked on that basis. The institutional-
ization and inertia, and the lack of major war, gradually
removed the sense of the dynamic interaction between the
political context and the instruments of power that is at the
heart of strategy. This dynamic was only experienced spas-
modically and at the margins of the cold war. Deterrence
might have begun after the Second World War as a particular means of persuading the Soviet Union not to start a third,
and could be considered as a type of strategic move that
might fit a variety of scenarios, but it eventually expanded to
take in the range of policies for managing the military dimension of the cold war. These policies were at times self-
contradictory and confused. They had simultaneously to
scare another superpower into acting cautiously while at the
same time rendering the superpower relationship less scary
and more reassuring.

The initial, rather simple formulation became complicated
by two developments. First, the circumstances which might

lead to an East–West clash took on increasing complexity, so the problem came to be posed in terms of managing crises rather than simply blocking aggression. Second, the Soviet Union acquired its own nuclear weapons, so the issue of when and how to initiate nuclear strikes was complicated by the probability of Soviet retaliation in kind. This became more complicated still with the arrival of thermonuclear weapons, which made possible 'city-busting' by a single weapon. It could be argued that the net effect of these complications was a grand clarification of the improbability of fighting a nuclear war and emerging as a viable society at its conclusion.

Nonetheless, refinements in the weapons, including munitions designed for battlefield use and missiles delivering warheads of ever longer range and improved accuracy, encouraged the belief that this improbability could be turned into a possibility. Strategists began to work out ever fancier forms of targeting designed to disarm an opponent before retaliation was possible or at least to knock him sufficiently off balance so that an advantageous diplomatic settlement might be reached. The scenarios they devised often managed to combine the most sophisticated technical analysis with the crudest psychological and political presumptions, so their influence on actual policy-making is still hard to discern.

In the 1960s the role of nuclear weapons in securing superpower restraint came to be recognized as 'mutual assured destruction'. So long as both sides were confident that they could inflict utter hell on the other, then a wider political equilibrium would be possible. There was, however, at the heart of this concept an awkward thought, which is why its critics seized on the acronym 'MAD'. If a nuclear war meant an inevitable slide into the ultimate catastrophe, then who would be irrational enough to set it in motion? Tom Schelling answered that this could come about through 'threats that leave something to chance', daring the enemy to recover a losing position by taking even greater risks. Such a situation conducive to irrationality would be generated. This raised the question of whether such a progressive loss of control might be set in motion by incidents that were comparatively trivial, marked by confusion rather than unremitting belligerence?[9]

So policies had to cover not only how nuclear weapons might be used in anger but also how they might be configured to send appropriately calming diplomatic messages to anxious allies, even as a steely resolve was being conveyed to adversaries. The deterrent threats might work best if there was a degree of automaticity in nuclear use, once the defined line of aggression had been crossed, yet every possible safeguard had to be in place to ensure no use when no line had been crossed, even though those in command had mistaken innocent or unrelated activities for hostile action. Automaticity had to be qualified to allow for the risk of poor control procedures combined with other technical and political mishaps. To reduce such risks, attention was given to ways by which international agreements might bring extra clarity, order and stability to the process. In short, and apart from occasional flurries, deterrence became not so much geared to the urgent avoidance of war as to the preservation of a sort of stability based on the fact that the nuclear age generated great wariness in the breasts of policy-makers.

Decline

In practice, the East–West strategic relationship in *all* its aspects carried sufficient disincentives to discourage precipitate action by either side. No political aspirations appeared to be worth total war. This strategic relationship turned out to be sufficiently robust in its essentials to survive new technologies and doctrines. With the stakes so high and the dangers so clear for all concerned, it is reasonable to suspect that nuclear deterrence was never truly tested, except perhaps in the early 1950s and early 1960s, although there was a flurry of tension and anxiety in the early 1980s. Then some senior people in the Reagan Administration talked as if they believed that a nuclear war might be lost and won, by deliberating on forms of nuclear employment, and some senior people in the Soviet Government took this conviction seriously. The existence of a usable nuclear arsenal provided reminders of the dangers of revived antagonism, but the practical difficulties of describing how it could ever be sensibly used discouraged recklessness. McGeorge Bundy, formerly President Kennedy's national security adviser, had long been dubious about the foreign policy value of extensive nuclear arsenals and concerned that the more esoteric strategic debates lost touch with reality. In 1983 he observed that: 'As long as each side has thermonuclear weapons that *could* be used against the opponent, even after the strongest possible preemptive attack, existential deterrence is strong and it rests on uncertainty about what could happen.'[10] This introduced the proposition that deterrence flowed not so much from specific preparations for employment or doctrinal pronouncements but from an overall sense that once any superpower war began there could be no knowing what might happen. As there was sufficient chance that the outcome would be catastrophic, it was best not to take the risk of finding out. This notion proved to be extremely seductive – not only because of its intuitive plausibility, but because it solved all those perplexing problems of nuclear policy by rendering them virtually irrelevant, so long as they did not stray too far into the realms of recklessness and foolishness. Although in policy-making circles it was still extremely difficult to think of ways to assess the size and composition of nuclear arsenals except by reference to the assumed requirements of actual exchanges, as evidenced in numerous debates in Washington over new weapons systems, these debates eventually required a routine quality. The scenarios were becoming drained of credibility as the original concept lost much of its intellectual rigour, while everything was still rationalized in terms of the requirements of deterrence.

Eventually, weariness began to surround deterrence, reflecting moral unease about such dependence upon threats of mass destruction and the nagging fear that even in the absence of any active belligerence on the part of either super-power, something could still go terribly wrong. A parallel history developed around the cold war, drawing attention to the possibility of hair-raising incidents in the event of misread messages, faulty early warning signals, pilots off course, poor communications and faults in command – any one of which might have triggered an inadvertent catastrophe. Calls grew for radical disarmament, although unless this was complete it was hard to guarantee safety, or else an attempt to find technical fixes to reduce the nuclear danger, of which the most notorious was President Reagan's strategic defence ini-tiative (SDI), based on the idea that it was better to 'protect than avenge'. Reagan was the first US President who did not really believe in deterrence, and became a not-so-closet nuclear abolitionist.

It is possible to chart the shifting attitudes towards deter-rence by examining the three great debates in the United States on ballistic missile defence. The first great debate, over 1965–72, concluding with the signature of the ABM (anti-ballistic missile) treaty, saw a system justified in terms of deterrence, and in particular one that protected the Amer-ican second-strike capability. The next debate, which lasted from 1983 to 1988, was prompted by President Reagan's strategic defence initiative. Here the rationale was anti-deterrence, at least on the President's part, although the project gained some support from those who believed that with a more modest objective it could serve deterrence. The Russians feared that it would support a first-strike capability but also, and more realistically, that by one way or another the US military would benefit from the stimulus given to new technologies. It was not the anti-deterrence rationale that undermined the project but its confused and futuristic quality, especially when it came to demonstrating what the system would actually protect. It required an enemy suffi-ciently threatening to warrant the effort but not so substan-tial as to overwhelm the proposed system, or clever enough to circumvent it. As such an enemy could not be guaranteed, the non-deterrence anti-offensive weapon rationale led naturally, including in Reagan's mind, to a case for abolishing all offensive weapons. If the aim was to protect rather than avenge, the disarmament solution made more sense than a hardware solution.

In the post-cold war world the demands might have seemed to be even less severe, perhaps even to the point of insignificance. Certainly, if deterrence was about nuclear weapons, then it was hard to see any conflicts around in which any interests, at least Western interests, would be sufficiently at stake to warrant issuing nuclear threats. Even with potential nuclear threats from relatively weak states that have yet even to demonstrate the requisite capability, there is strikingly low expectation that they can be dealt with through deterrence. This was evident in proposals for a national missile defence (NMD) system that gained prominence in the late 1990s. This had a much more modest objective than previous defensive systems, with neither Russia nor China as the focus, but other hostile states that were unable to take on the United States and its allies in regular battle and that were seeking their own minimalist form of nuclear deterrence. NMD was posed as a challenge to the growing dependence of weaker states on nuclear deterrence as a counter to the overwhelming conventional strength of the West. Without any suggestion that it might sustain Western deterrent strategies, NMD betrayed a lack of confidence in deterrence, specifically that in the face of clear threats (indeed complete elimination should they dare to mount some attack on the United States) certain states could be relied upon to act rationally. It also represented a challenge to the deterrent policies of others. If an interest in nuclear weapons of weak but 'rogue' states such as North Korea could be attributed to their lack of alternative means of persuading the United States to leave them alone, then a national missile defence system, if effective, could undermine their attempts at deterrence. This was to some extent how China, minded of its dispute with Taiwan, viewed the American programme, and it would be wrong to say that this was wholly absent in the Bush Administration's thinking, whatever was said officially. Russia, with its larger arsenal, could be more relaxed about NMD. Nonetheless, with their conventional forces in steep decline and the intentions of the West suspect, Russian generals concluded that they were bound to rely on nuclear deterrence.

Three Waves

It was therefore circumstances – there was nothing much that needed deterring – rather than questionable theory that was responsible for the eventual American shift away from a deterrence posture. Even so, the sustained intellectual critique left its mark and deterrence theory found itself in a damaged state.

As the cold war drew to a close, the essence of deterrence had become fuzzy, its boundaries increasingly elastic and the demands being placed on it expansive. The awkward doubts that had been articulated almost as soon as it was adopted as the official orthodoxy were no closer to being satisfied. Could deterrence be durable in either its extended or its mutual forms or be reliable in a crisis? Would it be eroded over the long haul? Could threats of denial be afforded? Could threats to punish in the face of equivalent threats of counter-punishment ever be credible? Theoretically, these doubts always appeared formidable, and so they stimulated considerable anxiety in policy-making circles, and restlessness in academic circles.

In the late 1970s, Robert Jervis identified 'three waves' of deterrence thinking in the USA. The first wave 'came and went in the early years of the nuclear era', including the pre-liminary writings of Bernard Brodie. Eventually, the over-bearing presence of nuclear weapons reinforced the view that total war could now only be threatened but never fought. This left behind the obvious thought that if nuclear war could not be fought, how could it be threatened? These thoughts were only explored in any depth, leading to the theoretical elaboration of the concept, following its adoption as the default strategy of the United States for the conduct of the cold war. Jervis called this the second wave, and it 'crested in the late 1950s'. The theory was developed through reflection on the twists and turns of East–West relations and, in particular, the impact of nuclear weapons and the gradual erosion of American superiority. Precisely because they were dealing with nuclear strategy, there was no basis for an inductive theory. 'Second-wave' theory was geared to operating within a reasonably stable bipolar relationship (though it did not necessarily feel so stable at the time) within which deterrence seemed to be a natural approach. By the time it entered its most creative phase, the critical commitments had been made and the essentials of a nuclear deterrence posture had been established. There seemed to be little point to theorizing about how a strategic relationship of this sort might come to be established in the first place when the core problematic was that it existed and somehow had to be survived. Theorizing was taken to a high level of abstraction, but no attempt was made to verify its central propositions until the 'third wave' began in the 1970s.[11]

By this time, the 'rational actor' model of decision-making, upon which deterrence appeared to depend, was under challenge in the academic community. There were all sorts of reasons to doubt the inevitable rationality of governments, let alone the extent to which they might usefully be viewed in a unitary form. Rationality was susceptible, in the new, vogue terminology, to 'groupthink', 'bureaucratic politics' and 'misperception'.[12] The more the literature of social psychology was examined, looking at threats from the perspective of the target, the less confidence there could be: 'Accumulating empirical evidence from laboratory experimentation suggests that decisionmakers systematically violate the strict behavioral expectations of rationality.'[13]

Academics, anxious to cut deterrence down to size, argued instead for a foreign policy based less on military threats and more on positive inducements and nuanced diplomacy, especially as the core East–West antagonism shrank in importance and the interests at stake in particular crises appeared to be more secondary than vital. In the first substantial 'third-wave' critique, based on case studies, Alexander George and Richard Smoke claimed that deterrence had led to an exaggerated role for the military dimension in US foreign policy and had discouraged attempts to transcend the cold war.[14] As the cold war concluded, Richard Ned Lebow and Janice Gross Stein summed up this line of thought, explaining how the United States had 'overdosed' on deterrence: distorting strategy by encouraging an exaggerated view of the importance of demonstrating 'resolve' in the face of challenges that would otherwise be recognized as minor; participating in an arms race; and aggravating and sustaining the degree of antagonism in the political relationship with the Soviet Union.[15]

So long as the focus was on deterring the Soviet Union and its allies, the analytical concerns could be dismissed as academic quibbles. It might not be known for certain that Moscow was being deterred, but this was not an area where many were inclined to take risks. Those who worried that measures taken in the name of deterrence could appear provocative occasionally got a hearing, but during the course of the cold war direct forms of communication between East and West offered means of providing reassurance that intentions were honourable and also helped reinforce the strategy by clarifying the areas where vital interests were at stake. With hindsight it is possible to identify moments when the reassuring messages were not getting through and relations were reaching a dangerous state. At the time, each side felt that its military posture was perfectly reasonable and not at all provocative.

The end of the cold war appeared to bring the debate on deterrence to a juddering halt. By the start of the 1990s the communists had lost their states, not to NATO aggression but to communism's own internal contradictions. The United States was left as the sole superpower. It no longer needed to fear challenges from the conventional military power of others. In the decade after the Soviet fall, liberal capitalism produced regular and impressive levels of economic growth, thereby apparently confirming the West's ideological superiority. Nuclear weapons would not play a central role in Western strategy: requirements could largely be met by conventional systems, so there was no need to rationalize their use. Deterrence was no longer needed. Even in East Asia, where communist parties retained their governing position, if not their ideological purity, international relations calmed down. New threats could be discerned. Here the problem was not so much would-be great powers challenging the status quo but, rather, a variety of delinquent states and shadowy terrorist groups, animated by vicious ideologies and deep hatreds. Clearly, classical deterrence was not going to work with such groups but that did not mean that the concepts could not be updated to cope with the new situation.[16]

When out of this tumult came a terrifying attack which caught the United States by surprise, President George W. Bush concluded that security threats such as these might not be deterrable at all. In a landmark speech of June 2002, he explained to the graduates of the US Military Academy, West Point, that they would fight the developing war on terror. They would confront an enemy that, unlike those of the past, lacked 'great armies and great industrial capabilities', but could get access to the most dangerous technologies. They might be 'weak states and small groups' intending to blackmail or harm the United States and its friends. The problem, according to Bush, was that such enemies could be beyond deterrence or containment because they have no 'nation or citizens to defend'. As the Administration concluded that pre-emption was a better way of dealing with such threats, many of those who had criticized deterrence before began to see merit in an approach that at least did not involve an early resort to war. The arguments of the critics were appropriated to help make the case not for more conciliatory policies, but for more robust ones. Charles Krauthammer chided the left for their conversion to a doctrine that they once deplored. He referred to 'deterrence nostalgics' who forgot their own earlier arguments about how close to the brink of

Armageddon the world had on occasion come during the cold war, or about the debilitating psychological effects of living under the nuclear cloud.[17]

Like all fallen kings, once toppled from its throne, deterrence appeared to be rather ordinary and dull. A good indication of its inherent dullness was the lack of movies made that showed deterrence at work. A number had been made about nuclear war (*Dr Strangelove, Fail-safe, War Games*). These normally revolved around the failure or near-failure of deterrence for reasons which appear to have little to do with international politics but rather with crazed leaders or with defects in systems designed to protect against unauthorized missile launches. One exception might be the quasi-documentary, *Thirteen Days*, dealing with the October 1962 Cuban missile crisis, which portrays the military as itching for war and applauds the cool politicians and diplomats for their appropriate combination of restraint and resolve. The only film entitled *Deterrence*, directed by Rod Lurie and released by Paramount to poor reviews in 1998, was also about a failure of deterrence, in this case another Iraqi invasion of Kuwait in 2007. It concludes with simultaneous nuclear exchanges which leave Baghdad vaporized and US cities surviving after weapons hit them but fortunately fail to detonate.

A doctrine that is so associated with continuity and the status quo, which occupies a middle ground between appeasement and aggression, celebrates caution above all else, and for that property alone is beloved by officials and diplomats, was never likely to inspire a popular following. Campaigners might march behind banners demanding peace and disarmament, the media might get excited by talk of war and conflict, but successful deterrence, marked by nothing much happening, is unlikely to get the pulse racing. It has no natural political constituency. As theory and practice, its best years appeared to be past, summed up by Colin Cray's reference to a condition of semi-retirement.[18] Does that mean it can be written off as a strategy of historical interest but no contemporary application?

2   THE MEANING OF DETERRENCE

To see whether deterrence as a strategic concept can be rescued from its cold war use and abuse, we need to return to first principles.

Deterrence is a coercive strategy. Elsewhere I have defined coercion as 'the potential or actual application of force to influence the action of a voluntary agent'. When the actions of a voluntary agent can be influenced without the threat of force, that involves *consent*; when the application of force is such that the agent can no longer be considered voluntary, that is *control*.[1] A coercive strategy involves the purposive use of overt threats of force to influence another's strategic choices. It presumes that the opponent will retain a capacity to make critical choices throughout the course of a conflict. By contrast, a *controlling* strategy involves the purposive use of armed force to restrict another's strategic choices, for example by defending disputed territory against any attempted seizure. A controlling strategy still depends initially on judgements concerning the opponent's strategy, but after a point that becomes irrelevant as the opponent runs out of options. A *consensual* strategy involves the adjustment of strategic choices with another without force or threats of force. Coercive strategies can be divided into the deterrent and the compellent, essentially between persuading another that they must not act for fear of the consequences if they do, and that they must act for fear of the consequences if they do not. Elements of all of these can be in play at the same time, either against a single opponent or against several opponents. Later I will consider whether compellence as a coercive strategy and pre-emption and prevention as controlling strategies are more relevant than deterrence for contemporary conditions.

Readers should be warned that this book explores a concept rather than tells a story and so at times it may seem rather abstract. I apologize for the appearance of entities known as A and B, occasionally joined by C, D and even E and F, who are so devoid of character. They are the best device I have found for illustrating points about strategic relations without getting lost in context – and in a short book that is important. Normally, A is the defender and B the challenger, but for reasons that become apparent these roles cannot always be assumed.

Strategic Deterrence

In the *Oxford English Dictionary* 'to deter' is defined as: 'To discourage or turn aside or restrain by fear; to frighten from anything; to restrain or keep back from acting or proceeding by any consideration of danger or trouble.' This reflects the normal implication of the statement 'A deters B', which is to view it from the perspective of A. A fears that B intends to act against its interests and takes steps to persuade B that this would be as unwise as it would be unwelcome. This is *strategic* deterrence. For our purposes, this can be described as a strategic option available to A which takes the form of an explicit commitment to take disciplinary action against B, if B acts in a specified manner against A's wishes. The word 'discipline' has the advantage of a dual connotation of both restraint and punishment. B should be convinced that any aggressive moves will fail to prosper either because of A's likely resistance or, even if they do prosper, because of retaliatory moves by A which will hurt B badly and far outweigh any prospective gains.

Much of the discussion surrounding deterrence considers threats of retaliation. If the presumption of a rationally determined self-interest was reliable, then this might be unproblematic, but it turns out to be difficult, if only because different actors have different views about what constitutes rational behaviour. For deterrence to work, A must persuade B to act to serve the interests of them both but according to the dictates of B's rationality. Even if A and B share the same framework of rationality, the persuasion might still fail because B may misinterpret the signals being sent by A or, if he understands them correctly, he may be unconvinced that A will implement any threats; and even if B *is* convinced, he may still believe that the costs will outweigh the prospective gains. A may be inarticulate; B confused. A tourist in a foreign country comes upon a policeman who is trying to tell him not to enter a restricted area. The language is unfathomable, the gestures confusing. The tourist walks on and is arrested. Deterrence has failed not because of wilfulness, or a cool calculation of risks, but because of complete incomprehension of the risks. Another tourist, this time from the same country, perfectly understands the policeman's message, but decides to reject it and is also arrested. The tourist claims he saw the stern admonitions accompanied by a friendly wink, and so decided that the threat was not serious. Maybe he was just fed up with being bossed about by authority figures and decided on the spur of the moment on a foolhardy gesture. Deterrence can fail because the target does not grasp the situation, or is inclined to foolish interpretations.

What is put into these threats may not be what is received. Examples can be found of misunderstandings and confusion which either fail to deter someone who needs deterring, or else aggravate a crisis that might have otherwise been managed peacefully. Military signals in particular are often notoriously ambiguous, and the problems of interpretation grow in the psychological intensity of crisis. So, even when all conditions for success are in place, and A has gone out of his way to empathize with B, the strategy can still fail because of eccentricities in B's decision-making processes or quite simple mistakes of interpretation and analysis. This is the gravamen of the complaint against deterrence: strategic theories that depend on the intelligence and rationality of others are unwise. But then, of course, so are theories which depend on assumptions of stupidity. All expectations of how another might take apparently simple decisions are subject to a finite margin of error, and the more complex these decisions, the greater the margin, and it becomes greater still the more one's own actions are a factor influencing those decisions. Some time ago Patrick Morgan made a valiant attempt to puncture this argument by drawing attention to the value of considering 'sensible' as opposed to 'rational' actors.[2] This lacks the analytical rigour offered by rational choice theory but may help us stay close to the methods through which choices are actually made. Many economists also now acknowledge that rationality is bounded and depends upon the circumstances or preferences of individual actors.

Proving that strategic deterrence works is particularly challenging. It is obvious when it fails. B has been told not to do X if he wishes to avoid dire consequences but X is nonetheless done. But when deterrence succeeds, all that is known is that X has not happened. That could be because B had never intended to do X in the first place, or was only suggesting he might for bargaining purposes. If he had the intention and then held back, this could be because of a whole range of factors, both internal and external. These might include the probability of being able to accomplish the act, the resources that would need to be expended, the opportunity costs, domestic opposition, problems of acquiring allies, local resistance and uncertainties over the benefits, as well as any dire threats of punishment. So deterrence might be tried as a strategy and fail – or be irrelevant, in that there was nothing to deter.

Internalized Deterrence

There is a quite different case, in which deterrence is not being deliberately applied as a strategy, yet it still succeeds.

If we return to the statement 'A deters B', we can see that it can also be interpreted from the perspective of B. Certain things are not done because, possibly without A knowing much about it, B has concluded that there is little to be gained and perhaps much to be lost by acting so directly against A's interests. B of course might be missing an opportunity because of mythical fears about the possible consequences. The condition of paranoia is an obvious example of being influenced by fear of another which has little basis in reality. A may remain innocent of his influence on B's calculations without the opponent losing his grip on reality. It is possible, indeed quite normal, to be persuaded against a particular course of action by the thought of how the target might respond. A would-be aggressor may thus be effectively deterred by an accurate assessment of the likely form of his potential victim's response without the victim having to do very much. In the policy debate, the phrase 'self-deterrence' was sometimes used to denote an unwillingness to take necessary initiatives as a result of a self-induced fear of the consequences. But all deterrence is self-deterrence in that it ultimately depends on the calculations made by the deterred, whatever the quality of the threats being made by the deterrer. The cowardly Falstaff's observation that the 'better part of valour is discretion' could be the motto of the congenitally deterred.[3]

Deterrence can seem far less problematic when we start from the point of view of the deterred. Once certain courses of action have been precluded through fear of the consequences should they be attempted, this conclusion may become embedded. It requires little further deliberation. In this way, at one level deterrence never goes away. Certain options – whole categories of actions – are precluded because of the possible responses of others. Land may be coveted but it is not grabbed; the unacceptable practices of foreign governments are denounced but they are left untouched; ideological ambitions are shelved; inconveniences, disruptions, outrages are tolerated; punches are pulled. Over time, after operations have been delayed and plans shelved, it is forgotten that these operations were ever proposed or that the plans were once taken seriously.

All this may happen without anyone who might have been the subject of these proposed moves issuing threats or doing much by way of military deployments. It simply results from the sensible application of what should always be the first principle of strategy: anticipate the probable responses of the opponent. This sort of deterrence is far more regular than the sort that captures the most attention from policy-makers and academics, when a determined effort is made to dissuade another party from taking action you judge harmful to your interests. Even when it takes this more engaged form, the act of deterrence may be no more than a hint here and a quiet word there, sufficient indication that the possibility of the offending act has been noted and preparations are being made. Only on occasion does it become necessary to move to the direct explicit threats tied to specified prospective acts commonly associated with a deterrence posture. This perspective is vital to any understanding of how deterrence might work as a political process. We can call it *internalized* deterrence.

The distinction can be explained if we consider a big man entering a bar. He might be timid and gentle, but his presence might still deter rowdy behaviour. Deterrence as a strategy, however, depends on the assumption that the behaviour of potentially hostile others can be manipulated through issuing timely and appropriate threats – so it would only be in play in this case if the big man comes in swaggering, glowering menacingly at possible trouble-makers and warning them to be good. Some conspicuous scars might help. Another example of internalized deterrence might be a threat issued by parents to their teenage children: 'Come home late again and you are grounded'. After a while the teenagers come home on time without their parents having to say a word. Only they know whether a deterrence relationship exists, whether they really would like to stay out longer yet fear their parents' response, but after a while the pattern of behaviour may be so internalized that there is no longer an issue. An actor may be deterred even if there is no direct interaction with the one doing the deterring, but in terms of strategy this is less significant than those cases where there is such an interaction. The problem, therefore, is not the existence of internalized deterrence – which happens all the time – but the development of strategies designed to produce a reliable deterrent effect. The challenge for strategic deterrence is to create internalized deterrence in its targets.

Constructing Threats

Strategic deterrence involves conditional threats, but the construction of those threats might vary according to what is to be deterred and how this is best achieved. Four important distinctions can be identified: narrow and broad, extended and central, denial and punishment, immediate and general.

Narrow and broad

Narrow deterrence involves deterring a particular type of military operation within a war, whereas *broad* deterrence involves deterring all war. From the start of the twentieth century, as it became apparent that some dreadful new types of weapon were becoming possible, there was a debate between those who sought ways to proscribe them (notably, for example, the Russian Tsar who promoted the first disarmament conferences) and those who seized on the idea that the more terrible wars became, the less governments would be willing to embark upon them. After the First World War, when 'poisoned gas' had been used, there were moves to ban the employment of such weapons in the future. In a 1925 protocol it was permitted to hold the weapons but not to use them, with the implication that any use would warrant an equally unpleasant retaliation and all would be losers. As the probability of strategic bombing was acknowledged during the 1930s a similar idea took hold – that so long as one side refrained from attacking cities, so would the other.

So narrow deterrence assumes that it is possible to deter a specific form of warfare even while other forms are progressing regardless. Restraint might be achieved through the threat of retaliation in kind, although this need not be the only explanation: the relative lack of utility of certain weapons (including chemicals) might be one reason and ethical considerations another. As was discovered during the Second World War, should utility become apparent, limits are hard to sustain. Germany first bombed European cities in the line of its army's advance but then attacked British cities as a form of coercion. By the time the British were in a position to respond with large-scale air raids of its own, it lacked alternative means of hurting Germany and so the air raids took place for want of anything better. Soon Germany was receiving terrible retribution. Japan also suffered terribly as a result of American raids against its cities, and eventually the release of two atom bombs.

From early on in the nuclear age consideration was given to the possibility that it might be possible to have a major war involving the great powers in which nuclear weapons would not be used. After the Korean War there was some hope that once it was accepted that an all-out war was unwinnable, then it would also follow that it would be impossible to pursue all-out objectives, as if the objectives set the tone for the conduct of war. Some toyed with the idea that limited use of nuclear weapons could be proportionate to limited political objectives. Either the so-called 'small' or 'tactical' nuclear forces could be employed to make up for deficiencies in conventional firepower and bolster the defence, or else it would be possible to move forward with graduated steps, steadily increasing the pressure on the enemy to cease his aggression. This approach depended on the assumption that there are distinct stages in war which could be well understood, and which would mean that the threat to move from one stage to the other would serve as a powerful deterrent and that, in the middle of events that would still be quite horrific, if not the worst imaginable, forms of compromise and bargaining would still be possible. Critics suggested that limits would be difficult to observe, even if at first only 'tactical' nuclear weapons were used, and that the belligerents could soon find themselves engaged in all-out nuclear war through the process that soon became described as 'escalation'. This raised the possibility that limited wars were best fought with conventional weapons and that nuclear weapons need have little strategic role other than the crucial one of deterring nuclear use by the other side.

This, however, went against the claim that it was the disproportionate nature of nuclear war that would deter potential enemies from aggressing in the first place. In the end, NATO adopted this notion of broad deterrence on the grounds that the best way to convince the Soviet Union not to aggress was to remove any doubt that the consequences would be horrific, even while accepting that the impact of nuclear war would be dreadful for all. When deterrence is discussed, it is often assumed that the objective must be to discourage all forms of warfare, and in particular aggression across recognized international boundaries, rather than a particular type of warfare. Yet it is still the case that even when war appears unavoidable, specific acts are often singled out as so changing the character of a conflict that they will prompt severe retaliation. Examples might be the use of weapons of mass destruction, any attack on civilians and extension of a conflict into adjacent territory. This should restrict the range within which hostilities might be conducted.

Extended and central

During the cold war the most troubling question was whether the United States was prepared to risk a nuclear catastrophe should Warsaw Pact armies break through NATO's defences and threaten to overwhelm its allies and gain control of all of Europe. The credibility of deterrence could not be separated from the political objectives it was supposed to support. Would the United States initiate nuclear war on behalf of third parties if unable to protect the American homeland against Soviet retaliation?

In a typology that never caught on, Herman Kahn, one of the most controversial second-wave theorists, distinguished three types of deterrence. Type I involved superpower nuclear exchanges; Type II involved conventional or tactical nuclear attacks involving allies; and Type III most other types of challenge.[4] The point was that at each stage the require-ments in terms of political will became more demanding, especially once both sides had acquired nuclear arsenals. It was one thing to threaten nuclear retaliation to deter nuclear attack. It was quite another to threaten nuclear use to deter a non-nuclear event, especially when the result could well be nuclear retaliation. Because it was always unlikely that the United States would be directly attacked by a major power other than by nuclear weapons – for unless either Mexico or Canada could be co-opted into an enemy alliance there was no basis for a land invasion – the most likely non-nuclear event to be deterred would be an attack on an ally. This came to be known as 'extended deterrence'. What Kahn described as Type 1 is probably best described as central deterrence.

Central deterrence was assumed to enjoy a higher credi-bility than extended deterrence. Attacks on sovereign terri-tory – the most vital of all vital interests – would provide sufficient motivation to order a nuclear riposte. With extended deterrence, on the other hand, it was necessary to be prepared to launch a nuclear attack in response to a conventional attack against third parties. The issue of extended deterrence arose because of the overseas commit-ments of the United States. Capabilities to attack the United States might exist, but it was only the extension of American interests that created potential conflicts with other powers. The limits to extended deterrence were a function of the strategic balance, which confirmed the risks of coming to the aid of allies, and the identification of the most vital allies for whom these risks might still be worth running. In principle, to be an ally of the United States might be thought sufficient to be considered a vital interest of the United States and so gain the benefits of deterrence. The model alliance was that of NATO, which brought in the key European allies, but this model was also applied to central Asia (CENTO) and south-east Asia (SEATO). For separate reasons there were alliances with Japan and South Korea, and in addition there was the close link with Australia and New Zealand (ANZUS).

The experience of SEATO and CENTO, both of which collapsed before the cold war was over, suggests that merely to declare alliance was not enough. Policy-makers were bound to make distinctions between the risks they were prepared to run and the resources they were prepared to devote, in different regions of the World. Western Europe, Japan and South Korea rated higher than other regions. The greater the vulnerability of the United States, the less likely it has appeared that it would take risks on behalf of allies. In this sense one might as usefully describe central deterrence as 'contracted' deterrence, to indicate shrunken political objectives or previously 'vital' interests being consigned to the periphery.

Denial and punishment

The problem of credibility was whether or not the opponent believed that threats would be enforced. This could be assumed to be linked to whether the issues at stake were worth the effort. Credibility was also assumed to be based on how past commitments had been honoured. This meant that once a commitment had been made, even if connected to a minor issue, then a new and possibly larger stake was created – whether a reputation for honouring commitments was being reinforced or undermined. It could also be assumed to be linked to the quality of the enforcement options, and in particular the ability of the opponent to resist enforcement and retaliate in kind.

The distinction between deterrence through *denial* and deterrence through *punishment* was first elaborated by Glenn Snyder in 1958.[5] Denial has coercive elements but essentially tends towards control – that is, the threat was to control the situation sufficiently in order to deny the opponent strategic options. In calculating costs, the opponent would have to consider those that would be incurred in the battle for control. Deterrence through punishment, by contrast, was pure coercion, in that the opponent was not denied choice, but was given powerful incentives to choose in a particular way. However, even with these strategies there were still costs to be incurred in creating the conditions in which there was no reason to doubt that the threats of pain could be realized.

Defences could be passive or active. Passive defences were also known as civil defences. In practice, in the face of nuclear attack, they involved running for shelter or evacuation and so were hardly passive. Active defences referred to the anti-aircraft or anti-ballistic missile systems designed to bring down the enemy offensive before any targets were reached. The problem, even combined with pre-emption, was that only a few nuclear weapons out of the hundreds (and eventually thousands) in existence could cause terrible devastation. Reliance on defences never really appeared as a credible option. In all the relevant calculations, the awesome power of individual weapons left little room for a margin of error. The speed of ballistic missiles meant that the time for decisions and their implementation would be compressed and possibly measured only in minutes.

The proponents of deterrence through denial during the cold war were not really thinking about defending against nuclear attack, although that was the thought behind President Ronald Reagan's proposed strategic defence initiative of the mid-1980s. Denial was really about boosting conventional defences on NATO's central front so that Warsaw Pact armies could not penetrate into Western Europe even if they wanted to. Despite the obvious merits of such an approach, in that the threat would be entirely credible and carry far fewer risks of a terrible escalation, it was always undermined by the cost that was expected to be involved in building NATO's forces up to Warsaw Pact levels, and also because, while denial was more credible, it was not necessarily so hazardous for the Warsaw Pact. It might be tempted to probe and push its luck knowing that the worst that could happen was that it would not make much progress. When faced with deterrence by punishment, calculations had to assume a devastating attack on the homeland rather than a stalemate on some distant battlefield. Even so, the punishment strategy was only adopted by NATO because of the lack of confidence in denial, as posing an insufficient threat to Moscow, and the high costs of reinforcing this strategy through an expansion of conventional forces. It was adopted when the United States still enjoyed nuclear superiority, though successive American governments came to regret the supreme risk that it obliged them to accept. In contrast to nuclear exchanges, a conventional battle in Europe would not threaten the homeland of either superpower.

With nuclear weapons in the background it was difficult for a distinctive body of conventional deterrence theory to develop. The most significant attempt to do so came from John Mearsheimer, who essentially argued that deterrence depended on the ability to convince aggressors that a military offensive, in the form of a blitzkrieg, would be frustrated. Samuel Huntington suggested that denial would not be enough and that an element of retaliation would also be needed to boost the threat (a potentially provocative notion in terms of military provisions at a tense time in the cold war). Looking specifically at the case of Israel, Jonathan Shimshoni made the case that a reputation can develop through repeated applications of force that eventually serves to have a deterrent effect.[6] The idea that occasional wars might be necessary to reinforce deterrence may be uncomfortable, but it does fit in with the notion of a 'costly signal', an action that simply because of the resources it demands undermines suggestions of irresolution. Reinforcement for this idea comes from both deductive and inductive theories.[7] For Richard Harknett, the key thing about conventional as opposed to nuclear deterrence lay not only in the certainty of catastrophe once nuclear weapons are used, but also in the high and contestable costs that conventional war involves. So conventional deterrence requires a demonstration of capability, while nuclear deterrence is more a matter of will. This creates a particular difficulty, in that providing the information to a potential aggressor about your ability to defend, necessary to make the threat credible, also may provide him with the information to circumvent the defence.[8]

In principle, denial is a more reliable strategy than punishment because, if the threats have to be implemented, it offers control rather than continuing coercion. With punishment, the target is left to decide how much more to take. With denial, the choice is removed. The comparative advantage of one over the other will in the end depend on the options available. These options may not be wholly distinct. Before B can be punished, A may have to defeat defending forces. Alternatively, causing severe losses amongst defending forces in pursuit of denial may cause punishment enough, leaving the target vulnerable against internal as well as external challenges. One way to think about this issue is to consider two types of costs with which A might threaten B: *resistance* costs and *compliance* costs. The former are those that will have to be incurred if A is to be prevented from implementing the threat; the latter are those that will be incurred should resistance fail. B has already begun to suffer before A is in a position to implement the core threat. Any coercive activity by A is likely to succeed when resistance costs exceed compliance costs for B. With denial, the two types of cost are directly related, in that, if resistance fails, compliance is automatic as success leads to effective control. With punishment, the two are separated, in that, even if resistance fails, control has not yet been achieved. Of course, at the same time, A must also accept costs, which can be described as the *enforcement* costs. If A's enforcement costs are high, then the value of B's compliance will need to be proportionately high. If enforcement costs promise to be essentially the same in both cases, then as far as A is concerned denial is preferable to punishment. The reverse will only be true when the enforcement costs associated with punishment appear to be significantly less costly and risky than those associated with denial. This was why NATO adopted a nuclear strategy in the face of the Warsaw Pact's conventional superiority.

Immediate and general

Another reason why a strategy of nuclear deterrence was adopted in the mid-1950s was a degree of confidence that it would not be put to the test. Instead of the Truman Administration's anxiety about a 'year of maximum peril', the Eisenhower Administration concluded that the Soviet Union was prepared for the 'long haul' and was not planning any early aggression. Deterrence at a time of crisis, a severe emergency when time is short and passions are high, involves *immediate deterrence*, described by Patrick Morgan as a relationship between opposing states where at least one side is seriously considering an attack while the other is mounting a threat of retaliation in order to prevent it. Morgan describes the alternative possibility as *general deterrence*, when opponents who maintain armed forces regulate their relationship even though neither is anywhere near mounting an attack. He notes that while general deterrence is more typical, the theory 'has been developed almost exclusively by hypothesizing an abstract world of immediate deterrence'. With general deterrence, the government of B might have been considering, perhaps without great conviction, the use of force against A, but it decides not to press on when it receives a rather vague threat from A. There is still the clear implication that without that vague threat B might have resorted to force.[9] This can be a stance of many years' duration. At some point the activity which prompted the original 'vague threat' might be forgotten. Over the intervening period, 'stopping short' would become institutionalized, so that it would take a deliberate decision by B to once again consider the resort to force and would require a reactivation of the threat by A to reconstitute deterrence. At the level of 'general deterrence', arms and warnings become part of the broad context of international politics, underpinning the system within which the state seeks its security. The idea is to manage the context so that for an opponent it will appear basically unattractive to resort to force.

The difference between general and immediate deterrence can be understood in terms of the degree of strategic engagement between A and B. Immediate deterrence involves an active and urgent effort by A to deter in the course of a crisis when the efficiency of any threats will soon be revealed by B's actual behaviour. General deterrence is altogether more relaxed: A conveys a sense of risk to B to ensure that active hostilities are never seriously considered. The lack of direct engagement means that deterrence depends largely on B's assessment of its strategic environment. General deterrence may become frail at times of revolutionary change or when the international order appears illegitimate in the eyes of rising states. History is therefore full of cases in which general deterrence, in the guise of a balance of power, has broken down. However, it did not do so when the balance was based on nuclear power and, over time, rather than tending towards a revival of immediate crisis, despite some tense moments, it tended instead towards consensual relations.

The workings of general deterrence – if that adequately describes the cold war relationship for most of the time – seem to have involved the internalization of certain dangers by policy-makers. There was no need for explicit threats; indeed, to the extent that they were explicit, they were routine and non-specific, working side by side with other more cooperative activities or just deliberate efforts not to get in each others' way. Such an arrangement might cease to function as the relationship became essentially non-antagonistic, reflected in a dissolution, or, at least, an erosion, of alliances – as happened at the end of the cold war. Alternatively, there might be a move towards immediate deterrence. If, while the war is still only a distant threat, but is nevertheless conceivable, a relationship becomes unstable and looks like breaking down, then a concern with regard to capabilities for immediate deterrence may develop, and this in turn could aggravate the relationship. Prior to that point the policy problem is to maintain options for the contingency of immediate deterrence in a political climate created by years of general deterrence. Capabilities may well deteriorate, with the only possible consolation being a comparable deterioration in those of the adversary. At times of general deterrence, each side's force structure will be shaped by a variety of economic, technical, cultural and political factors as well as an assessment of the other's force structure. In times of immediate deterrence, states become more concerned about military efficiency and combat readiness. If A's front-line forces have declined too far in relation to B's, then there is a risk of even a mild crisis being aggravated by a frantic rush to get forces in place.

General deterrence involves an institutionalized perception by a state or group of states that, despite continuing antagonism, it should not expect to be able to resolve its disputes with another state or group of states by military means. This will reflect an understanding of the vital interests of the deterrer which the deterred accepts must be respected. The longer this condition lasts, the more stable it is likely to become, with a growing tolerance of disparities in military capabilities and also of political change, tending towards the dissolution of antagonism. Political change that aggravates the antagonism will produce instability and a tendency towards crisis, and the consequent practice of immediate deterrence.

Unpacking the concept of deterrence in this way explains why it is so hard to pin down. For students of international relations this can be very frustrating because of the limits placed on its explanatory value. We come here to a fundamental question of methodology. Those who wish international relations to be a true social science seek propositions that can be validated through an empirical investigation. A reliable theory will offer confidence that if certain conditions are present a given outcome will follow. The challenge lies in identifying a dependent variable to be explained, the causal or independent variables that provide the explanations, and the mechanisms or causal logic which link the two.[1] At first glance, deterrence theory appears to offer propositions that might be tested in this manner, and the attempt to do so has been the basis of much 'third-wave' theorizing. *When Does Deterrence Succeed and How Do We Know?* asked Richard Ned Lebow and Janice Gross Stein. 'My objective', explained Paul Huth, 'is to formulate and then empirically test a set of hypotheses on the political and military conditions under which deterrence is likely to succeed or fail.'[2]

For students of strategy there is a problem even with the objective of creating general propositions establishing close causal relationships between independent and dependent variables. The essence of strategy is that it involves interdependent decision-taking. The strategy of A depends on an assumption about the likely strategy of B, which in turn anticipates A's strategy and so on. There can therefore be no clear-cut distinction between the independent and dependent variables. If A can move effortlessly into a controlling position, with overwhelming force, B's strategic choices will become virtually irrelevant. Deterrence, however, is coercive, and that means that B will remain an independent agent. In addition, it is about threats of force as much as applications, and there is plenty that can be contested when assessing the credibility and quality of threats.

If true theory requires that the critical variables be defined with sufficient precision to be recognizable and then measurable, problems will arise if a critical variable defies these requirements and frustrates comparisons with other possibly important variables. The more variables involved, the harder this task becomes. To cope with this complexity, it helps to have a large number of cases in which the key variables are in play, but on many vital topics in international affairs there is simply an insufficient number of cases, even when looked at over time and involving many different parts of the world. The third-wave theorists put a considerable effort into seeking evidence from cases where challenges to the status quo had been faced and either successfully or unsuccessfully rebuffed. One approach, exemplified by the work of Alexander George, takes a few cases where there are possibilities of structured comparisons and examines them in depth.[3] Because of the relative paucity of comparable cases, this approach cannot prove any propositions, although it can disprove some. The advantage is that it adds to our understanding of the cases in question and, more generally, of how strategic choices present themselves to policy-makers and why and how they make their choices. The more ambitious inductive theorists seek far and wide to gather a sufficiently large sample, but recasting these cases into a form suitable for rigorous analysis requires them to be extracted from their context. When the cases are chosen from separate incidents from different regions and at different stages in the development of the international system, the search for statistically significant correlations is likely to be skewed.[4] With deterrence, there was always the risk that important cases could well escape notice because, if successful, nothing much had happened. In practice, the result is apt to be either bland or riddled with exceptions. Even when the analysis is quite exemplary, the conclusions may not survive the next case. If there is a variable, which could determine whether deterrent strategies can succeed, it is properly described as 'elusive', and the search for it may have been unavoidably futile. This is the problem with international relations theory masquerading as science: too many variables; too few cases.

There would be few instances in which it could be asserted with confidence that B reconsidered an original intention to act in a particular way *solely* because of a conditional threat issued by A. Lebow and Stein picked what they considered to be a critical area: 'immediate extended deterrence'. This would occur 'only when an attacker contemplates military action against another country and a third party commits itself to the defense of the country threatened with attack'. To be sure of such cases, independent evidence was required of a would-be challenger's intentions, and the defender must have defined the unacceptable behaviour, made public the commitment to punish or restrain aggressors, demonstrated the resolve to do so and possessed even rudimentary capabilities to implement the threat.[5] These were demanding criteria.

In terms of empirical research, it has always been even more difficult to ascertain whether general as opposed to immediate deterrence is actually operating. We can assume that when immediate deterrence becomes necessary, and is successful, it may represent a failure in general deterrence, suggesting that the variables that influence particular outcomes in one type of deterrence will not necessarily be relevant for another. Lebow and Stein acknowledge that those interested in exploring general deterrence are deprived of an 'evidentiary trail' and lack clear criteria for case selection, which is why 'analysts of deterrence generally restrict their selection to cases of immediate deterrence'. One problem is that general deterrence lasts for an extended period. Some inductive theorists attempted longitudinal studies in which deterrence relationships of long duration were considered, but this required understanding the range of independent factors working on both parties over time, as well as the interaction between the two.[6] The processes of learning turn out to be complex, and messages about another's resolution may be acquired in only a partial, limited and slow fashion.[7] Thus, the sort of theorizing that might be most help in analysing the processes of internalized deterrence has been the least developed in the strategic studies literature.

This reflected the wider problem in extracting moments of deterrence out of their wider political context and separating them from the stream of history. It is not always clear in particular situations who is challenging and who is defending, and designating parties as one or the other may be no more than a partisan judgement. Here, structured case studies can be helpful. The theory suggested a support for the status quo against a revisionist power, but case studies demonstrated just how subjective a concept the status quo could be, to the point where both protagonists could claim to be acting in its support, and could also fail to understand why the other side could claim otherwise. George and Smoke had warned that it would be difficult to develop a general prescriptive theory as if deterrence was a 'separable, self-contained phenomenon'. Following this, Lebow and Stein wanted to see deterrence considered 'as an integral part of a broader, multi-faceted influence process'.[8]

Lebow and Stein criticized second-wave theorists for concentrating on how to communicate to the prospective aggressor an intent to protect a nation believed to be at risk without examining too carefully how the intent to protect a vulnerable nation had been formulated in the first place, and how the capabilities to back this up had been acquired and developed. Jervis agreed: second-wave theorists had been over-impressed by 'strategic interests' (the 'degree to which a retreat would endanger the state's position on other issues') and the more tactical 'commitments' (the means by which states manipulate situations to make it harder for themselves to retreat and persuade the opponent to concede). Instead, he stressed the importance of 'intrinsic interests', which 'represents the inherent value that the actor places on the object or issue at stake'.[9] When George considered why, at times, strong powers had failed to coerce the weak, asymmetrical motivations also loomed large.[10] The extent to which the issues at stake mattered to the parties affected the extent to which they were prepared to suffer to protect their interests. If anything, these interests represented the most likely independent variable, but they were not fixed. How much they mattered as a whole, and the weight to be attached to the individual elements that made them up, could often only be realized during the course of a conflict in which they were under threat.

Multiple Audiences

Deterrence, therefore, does *not* refer to a type of strategic relationship between A and B, but only to one aspect. Most strategic relationships are extremely complex and are unlikely to be controlled by a single type of communication, however severe its implications. The fact that the cold war involved a bipolar relationship allowed for deductive theorizing. The situation to be examined was stark and simple. There was, however, an inherent unreality in the presumption of a dyadic relationship involving only two actors, A and B (in practice, the United States and the Soviet Union). The circumstances in which threats were issued and received, even during the cold war, were far more complex. To understand how deterrence is likely to work in practice, we need to have a sense of how this political context impacts on the formulation of strategic threats.

It is often suggested, for example, that governments on occasion talk up the possibility of war and create an artificial sense of crisis in order to mobilize public opinion, unify an

otherwise divided country and wrong-foot domestic opponents. The whole exercise may be designed to strengthen the
position of an otherwise shaky regime, in circumstances
where there is no real danger. Yet a government might claim
that the very possibility of danger could be justification
enough, because it has encouraged people to be better prepared than they might otherwise have been and has alerted
others to the seriousness of the situation – for example,
potential allies and international bodies. A may threaten B
with retaliation if C is attacked. B may protest that he has
no intention of attacking C. Perhaps this is so. It does not
matter. C has reason to be grateful to A and reason to hope
that a message has been sent to B that will remain relevant
over the long term. With luck, D, E and F have also been
impressed and will adjust their expectations accordingly in
their future dealings with both A and B. When India resumed
nuclear testing in 1998, it claimed that this had been
prompted by concern over China, although it was widely
assumed that the main purpose was to keep Pakistan in its
place. Others suspected that the main concern was to shore
up domestic support. Pakistan might have seen an opportunity to get other great powers to take a keen interest in its
security in return for not testing its own weapons. Domestic
politics demanded that it tested. Similarly, North Korea's
moves to rationalize its own nuclear programme were initially linked to Japan, although the Americans assumed that
they were the real targets. Analysts suggested that the move
had something to do with the North's economic condition
and was designed to sustain a crisis atmosphere as well as
create a bargaining position for future economic assistance.
Nonetheless, if the programme was taken too far, non-nuclear
Japan might have to consider how to respond. The USA
might see this as an attempt to break out of containment and
therefore act to put it back. Who is attempting to influence
whom, and for what purpose, is rarely straightforward.

Much is made of the problems likely to result from a
failure to communicate effectively to those who are supposed to be being deterred. Yet describing what is to be

deterred and how it is to be deterred in terms that are fully understood by friends, allies and constituents makes perfect strategic sense, especially if their support may be vital in a coming trial of strength – even if the net effect on the actual opponent may be to confuse rather than to clarify, to provoke rather than to dissuade. Multiple audiences are being addressed all the time. There are a number of reasons why a deterrence strategy might be followed, even if the danger from the opponent is insufficient to justify the threats, the threats are recognized at the time to be insufficient to deter the opponent, or it is understood that this can only be one element in overall foreign policy or crisis diplomacy. They will influence the attitudes and behaviour of anyone who is aware of them, and so they must be framed with this in mind. Formal deterrence theory must take an austere view of threats issued to impress audiences other than the notional target. As a result, it may not be able to begin to make sense of the political processes at work.

It may well be, as Keith Payne argues, that American policy-makers fall into the trap of confusing rationality with reasonableness, so that when adversaries fail to act as intended, or the theory predicts, they appear as irrational.[11] This takes us back to the problem of rational decision-making which in the end requires us to accept that an actor can be rational within his own framework of understanding, though that framework may differ markedly from our own. The point here, however, is that at least in the first instance a strategic discourse is bound to be phrased in terms that make most sense to those who must be persuaded of its wisdom. This may well assume norms and standards of reasonableness that lay the ground for later misapprehensions and miscalculations. A different sort of problem may emerge if the opponent understands only too well what is being said, for the need to discuss openly a proposed strategy provides valuable guidance to the opponent on how that strategy might be defeated.

This explains why acts of deterrence may appear unsuccessful yet serve strategic purposes all the same. As the drama and intensity of an immediate crisis subside, policy itself may begin to drift away from a primary concern with the attitudes and behaviour of the adversary and towards the need to reassure domestic opinion and allies of one's responsibility and commitment. The process might then become circular. As military deployments and public declarations reflect these considerations, and progressively less attention is paid to their impact on the adversary, then there is a risk of conveying impressions of either indifference or provocation, thereby resulting in a return to crisis.

The danger for the decision-maker is that policy becomes so geared to satisfying the vigorously communicated needs of those close at hand that insufficient account is taken of the needs of those more distant and less insistent. The hierarchy of concerns on the foreign policy agenda will reflect hierarchies within national political systems and salient alliances and international organizations. There are those whose position is such that their anxieties cannot be ignored, even if they verge on the paranoid. Others may discern risks accurately but must struggle to be heard, like Cassandra of Troy, who was given the gift of prophecy combined with the curse of never being believed. At times of peace, when it is difficult to assess with confidence one perception of security vulnerabilities against another, the tendency for the matter to be decided by sheer political weight will be accentuated. Domestic consensus or alliance solidarity may be happily mobilized behind a set of propositions that have passed no test other than political acceptability. More seriously, military provisions may well follow these propositions. C is important to A and knows how to make a fuss, but D is of little consequence. It is therefore natural to make provision to defend C but do little for D. But if, as far as the adversary B is concerned, D is exactly what is in dispute and C is irrelevant, then a crisis might emerge in the very area where A is least prepared. Because military resources have been allocated to C at the expense of D, B has been provided with an opportunity. A must then decide whether anything can be done about D and this means that he is obliged to clarify his interests in D with regard to both dispensability and the resources that are worth expending on its behalf, supposing that sufficient, appropriate resource can be shifted back to D in time to prepare some defence. While playing for time with B, A may make promises to D that cannot truly be kept. Such connections may help explain why governments still insist on adopting hawkish postures when entering disputes where the balance of power is against them, and the apparently stronger party also cares more about the matter at hand. In such cases there may be reasonable grounds for predicting unsuccessful deterrence, but, unless one assumes that the inevitable loser is simply a victim of poorly informed theory, the explanatory task requires attending to the complex strategic relations that have left A looking the wrong way.

Patrick Morgan has followed through the logic of those studies of deterrence which have sought to address its psychological aspects, which, he suggests, should lead to treating deterrent behaviour as an extension of the 'nature and character' of the state involved:

> How a state practises deterrence would tell us as much or more about the state itself than it does about the state's opponents and the threats they pose. It is possible that deterrence behavior is nor primarily a reflection of opponents and threats, which would help explain why deterrence is sometimes inappropriately practised. If internal factors drive the specific application of deterrence as much as or more than external threats, there is apt to be a frequent mismatch between the external realities with which deterrence is expected to cope and the ways in which it is undertaken.[12]

He then explains features of the US approach to deterrence by reference to such factors among policy-makers as a fear of a reversion to isolationism, the strength of right-wing politicians and their possible reaction to foreign policy reverses, and the need to reassure wavering allies. This raises, he concludes, the intriguing possibility that US deterrence posturing has often been aimed at domestic, not just foreign, targets: that US governments have often sought credibility abroad when a major objective was to reassure their own citizens. Morgan adds that this may be unavoidable when practising deterrence in an open, democratic society.[13] It is my argument that such considerations should not be seen as aberrant, distorting factors, or just as consequences of particular strategic cultures, but as a natural consequence of the multiple pressures working on any collection of decision-makers and their need to fashion policies which meet both functional and political criteria, though these are often contradictory in their implications.

Indeed, as the greatest uncertainty is likely to surround the opponent, it is quite reasonable to construct a strategy that is at least sensitive to the choices being faced by those closer to home. As a crisis unfolds, the decision-makers should become clearer about their own interests at stake as well as those of all other parties, including their main opponents, and likely patterns of behaviour. In these circumstances a conditional threat need not be an exclusive strategy, but may supplement promises of rewards and active negotiations, as well as complement preparations to decide the matter through force of arms if all else fails.

Reputations

Another complicating factor is the impact of one act of deterrence for those that might follow. In principle, every act of foreign policy has some significance for the creation of expectations of future performance. Compliance may be a form of humiliation and an acknowledgement of submission. This can have long-term consequences. How one deters now will have an impact on how much one might have to deter in the future. As a result, when a crunch point is reached in a crisis, when prudence and caution might argue for avoiding a confrontation or not enforcing a demand, thought must be given to the implications of this for crises to come. If the idea gains hold that you have a natural tendency to back away, then you will appear less dependable to allies and a soft touch to adversaries. The most notorious statement of this view came from Tom Schelling, who wrote that 'face' is 'one of the few things worth fighting over'. Though 'few parts of the world are intrinsically worth the risk of serious war by themselves, especially when taken slice by slice', he acknowledged, nonetheless, that 'defending them or running them may preserve one's commitments to actions in other parts of the world and at later times'. 'Face', he continued, 'is merely the interdependence of a country's commitments; it is a country's reputation for action, the expectation other countries have about its behaviour.'[14]

The risk involved in this logic lay in creating a vital interest where none truly existed, for example by presuming that commitments were invariably interdependent, so that once a state retreats on one issue, this must undermine its ability to stand firm elsewhere.[15] It might, as Morgan noted, be the case that commitments involving nuclear weapons could only be made credible through technical measures, for no political commitments could ever be convincingly demonstrated to be worth nuclear war. This created a bizarre logic which leads to a rational decision to cultivate an image of recklessness and irrationality. Morgan cites Earl Ravenal's *reductio ad absurdum*: 'In order to buttress its credibility, a nation should intervene in the least significant, the least compelling, and the least rewarding cases, and its reaction should be disproportionate to the immediate provocation or the particular interest at stake.'[16] This aspect of Schelling's theory was, from the start, a target for his critics, not least because of what appeared to be its consequences in Vietnam. The empirical analysis gave it little support. Huth found no evidence to suggest that losing a war against one country led another to assume a lack of resolve against them.[17] Reputation is intangible and difficult to measure and identify. It provides an intuitive test of the quality of a policy rather than a specific goal in itself.

Jonathan Mercer has explored this issue. He defines a reputation as 'a judgement of someone's character (or disposition) that is then used to predict or explain future behaviour'. A disposition to behave in a particular way is rarely the only explanation of particular behaviour. There will also be situational attributes, the circumstances that reduce our options and point us in a particular direction, whatever we might be inclined to do if the choice were free. These situational attributes are discounted when considering another's reputation, and Mercer provides evidence from a number of case studies to show that, by and large, adversaries are assumed to be resolute and allies irresolute, so that evidence to the contrary is given situational explanations. There is therefore no direct correspondence between behaviour and reputation. Mercer concludes that while deterrence theorists advise policy-makers to pay now to avoid future costs, this is pointless because there probably will not be any future costs: 'fighting to create a reputation for resolution with adversaries is unnecessary, and fighting to create a reputation for resolution with allies is unwise.'[18]

Mercer's analysis, considering how others are perceived rather than how they wish to be perceived, is convincing as far as it goes and it contains a wise caution for the over-excited policy-maker. It highlights the extent to which dispositional attributes, questions of character, are tricky issues for deterrence theorists. 'Face' or 'reputation' may not be such foolish motives, but they cannot be detached from the immediate problem at hand, or considered separately from performance. They are poor reasons for persevering with a failed policy instead of managing a prudent change of course, which in the long run might have spared a reputation. In understanding why this might happen, as in Vietnam, we must return to the problem of multiple audiences. Mercer considers the differential effect of the same behaviour on adversaries and allies, but there will also be a critical audience at home. The quality of political leadership will be closely scrutinized and few politicians wish to acquire a reputation for irresolution in defence of national interests. Though he shows how hard it is to change assumptions about the dispositions of others, Mercer does not explain the additional problem of how they came to be established in the first place.[19]

The relevance of the critique for deterrence theory is also mixed. To be strict, deterrence theory depends on situations producing reasonably predictable outcomes rather than dispositions. Because each situation is different in international affairs, the conclusions drawn from one incident may have little relevance for another. So Mercer is right to criticize the notion that resolution in one crisis begets a reputation for resolution that will be helpful in the next, but this may not be because of the way that reputations are formed. If it is accepted that the dispositions of B are important, so that it cannot be guaranteed to respond to a standard stimulus in a standard way, then A must tailor threats (and inducements) accordingly, drawing on what is known empirically about B. Assumptions will have to be made about character, and these must come from somewhere. That is, states, like individuals, do have reputations, and while they may be impervious to deliberate manipulation (as individuals also often find, despite the interventions of PR specialists), there is no reason to suppose that past impressions are irrelevant. It is clearly not the case, for example, that enemies of the United States have always thought of it as being resolute. They have often assumed irresolution on the basis of evidence of squeamishness in the face of casualties.

Hopf provides an interesting take on this issue. He has also provided a sustained critique of Schelling's propositions on reputation, in his case by looking at cold war conflicts in the third world and the impact on Soviet views of US resolve. The problem, he notes, is not one of deterrence failing because of misperception or poor information processing, but of deterrence succeeding with far less effort than commonly supposed. 'In a nutshell', he argues, 'convincing a challenger that a defender is credible and that regional actors are going to resist is a far easier task than the theory assumes.' What happened in the periphery of the third world had no relevance for what Moscow thought would happen in the event of a major European conflict. More seriously, even in these contexts, the USA had a strong hand to play – it just did not always take the form of military instruments. Often the most important factors, especially in areas where the most vital interests were not at stake, were economic and diplomatic instruments, and these could be used to create a reputation for resolve. Hopf therefore argues that 'deterrence theory must expand its scope to capture an array of deterrent instruments that the theory's focus on military tools omits'.[20]

Challenger and Defender

Classical deterrence theory has also been charged with unreality in the formulaic dichotomy that divides protagonists into challenger and defender. Lebow has also looked at the social psychological literature and noted just how rarely the actors see themselves in the terms that the theory would suggest, or as they are described by the other. This affects the communication between them, so that threats that A has constructed with great care still turn out to be over- or under-interpreted by B, as preludes to aggression or bluffs designed to impress a domestic audience. Lebow argues for alternative strategies of reassurance:

> Unlike deterrence, they root the source of overt, aggressive behaviour in the acute vulnerability of adversaries. Reassurance encourages self-defined defenders to search for effective ways of communicating their benign and defensive intentions to would-be challengers. They do so to reduce the fear, misunderstanding and insecurity that are so often responsible for conflict escalation. The combination of carrots and sticks is often more successful than either alone.[21]

If the signals sent in coercive threats are rarely transparent, prone to misinterpretation and highly dependent on context, then Lebow proposes that the bargaining process inherent in coercive activities (in that they do not assume the elimination of the protagonist but only a more favourable relationship) could be achieved through direct communication,

allowing the protagonists to negotiate on their understand-
ings of the context, including the origins of a conflict, respec-
tive motives and views about what is at stake.

The most thorough study of the role of inducements as an
alternative to deterrence is Stephen Rock on appeasement.
Appeasement has a much worse reputation in international
affairs than deterrence, because of the failure of the democ-
racies to buy off Hitler at Munich. As Rock notes, few would
argue that it could serve as the foundation for a theory of
universal applicability. Even so, as he shows, the record of
appeasement, defined as a policy of 'reducing tension with
one's adversary by removing the causes of conflict and dis-
agreement' is not bad, and the consequences are often preferable to deterrence. This clearly will not work if war is part
of the adversary's strategy, but it might when threats of force
are instrumental and the inducements on offer have some
appeal. Rock sees levels of greed and insecurity as important
variables, creating more problems the higher they are.[22]

Reassurance does not, however, necessarily need to be an
alternative to conditional threats: it can be a complement. It
also seems to be as unlikely as deterrence to serve as an invin-
cible strategy on its own. Reassurances are, after all, regular
features of all social discourse and suffer from problems
similar to those of deterrence. A may seek language to
reassure B but instead finds idioms and metaphors that are
alarming; even if perfectly understood, the message may not
be taken at face value but is assumed to be there for form's
sake rather than because it reflects a genuine intention;
hidden agendas may be detected lurking behind particular
messages, especially if it becomes noted that others are
getting different messages; past reassurances that have turned
out to be misleading will mean that new reassurances are
discounted. So what starts as a reassurance may be received
as a threat.

All these studies draw our attention to the need to consider strategic relationships in the round, and to take account
not only of the messages delivered by A but also of those
actually received, and then delivered in turn, by B. The basic

conclusion, as before, is that policy-makers need to read situations and tailor their policies carefully. It is not surprising
that one survey of the field concludes that 'cognition is a critical variable in understanding international affairs, perhaps
even as important as interests and capabilities in terms of
providing insights into the dynamics of international
processes'.[23] This is not to argue that all communications are
doomed to fail, and that actors in international affairs rarely
understand each other, although this is an impression that
can at time be conveyed by the literature in the field most
concerned with cognition. As Jervis observed, noting the
routine nature of misperception in international affairs: 'It is
hard to find cases of even mild international conflict in which
both sides fully grasp the other's views.'[24] Partial grasps of
reality are the norm for us all, and fortunately can be sufficient. If it is the case that the most effective communications
are going to be those based on a most careful interpretation
of the available evidence and a keen sense of context, then
it is likely, as much of the work discussed in this section
demonstrates, that the most useful scholarly contributions to
the subject will come from a few rich case studies. These may
not generate a general theory, but they might at least alert
academics and policy-makers to the sort of factors that could
be vital when loosely comparable cases arise in the future.

In their rigorous defence of rational deterrence theory,
Achen and Snidal draw attention to the pay-off between
deductive power, which requires parsimony in assumptions,
and historical accuracy.[25] So the fact that mental calculations
made by actors draw them away from what might be pre-
dicted by a deductive theory does not invalidate the theory,
because all the theory can offer is propositions on the choices
available and the variables that might influence the choices.
Deductive theory can cope with the perverse calculations of
decision-makers in practice, even if habitually deviant, for it
can at least be useful to the analyst to know what actors
might be expected to do in particular situations if their information was good and their reasoning displayed a modicum
of rationality. The problem is whether it is possible to be both

parsimonious and at all relevant as the situations to be studied become ever more complex, involving many actors, diverse interests, domestic as well as external, plus many forms of communication, reassuring as well as threatening, and then a sense of the impact of the outcome of each crisis on the one to follow. In these circumstances there may be no obviously rational courses to follow, against which actual practice might be measured.

So where does this leave us? Strategic deterrent threats may be issued by A for a variety of reasons, not all connected with the allegedly intended behaviour of B, and so not surprisingly may not make much impact either way on B. Nonetheless, they can meet other political goals which matter to A. At the same time, B might be deterred by A, for reasons that have little to do with anything recently and explicitly said or done by A. Internalized deterrence works through an appreciation of how A might respond (possibly with C, with or without D), using both consensual and coercive means, to particular acts by B. With all this in mind, B must then make a judgement as to whether this is a risk worth taking, and whether he might start issuing some coercive threats or reassuring promises of his own. If strategic deterrence is to be relevant, somehow A needs to understand how B constructs reality and find ways of manipulating these constructions, while at the same time addressing the concerns of all those other, more friendly, actors whose strategic interests he is bound to take into account. There are limits to the extent to which a deterrent effect can be contrived independently of a sense of the interests involved (which are themselves not fixed but can change over time). A deterrent effect may be created by putting these interests at risk through threats of armed force, but also non-military measures, and can be reinforced by a variety of economic and political inducements and reassurances.

4 NORMS AND CRIMINALITY

The Criminological Contribution

While the evidence-based literature on this matter in strategic studies is limited by restricted comparability of available case studies, issues of strategic and internalized deterrence can be explored further through the criminological literature. As already noted with Bentham, this is where the debate on deterrence began. What is striking is how similar the debates are in the strategic studies and criminological communities, yet how little they draw upon each others' work.

To start with, there is deterrence through both denial and punishment. With crime prevention, deterrence is discussed in terms of denying criminals opportunities – placing security guards at doors, keeping windows locked and alarms activated, paying attention to issues of personal safety. All these measures may be deterrent if they demonstrate that the criminal act is apt to fail. In circumstances where the possibilities for denial are limited and a degree of vulnerability is unavoidable, then deterrence has to work through the threat of punishment, which in turn requires that there is a significant likelihood of any culprit being apprehended, brought to trial, being found guilty, and then receiving a sentence, whether a fine or custody, that will make an impression not only on their future behaviour but on the behaviour of others who might be similarly inclined. Bentham was even interested in the possibility of influencing would-be offenders through creating the impression of pain without actually having to inflict it.

The eighteenth-century Italian philosopher Cesare Beccaria, who influenced Bentham, saw the proper design of punishment as being critical to effective deterrence, with the key qualities being that it should show certainty and celerity. To this day, this provides the essential framework within which criminological investigations into deterrence are pursued.[1] These empirical studies have taken off since the 1960s, in part as a result of the debate on the death penalty. Before that, other than accepting that the very existence of a criminal justice system prevented a complete descent into anarchy, research concentrated on the psychological and social factors that determined propensities to offend. There was less interest in the offender's own risk calculus and how it might be affected at the margins by the prospect of punishment.

The question of murder and capital punishment has been a continuity in this debate, again going back to Beccaria. He put particular stress on swift justice because he believed that it was important to establish a close association between crime and punishment. He was far less impressed with the case for severe punishment, on the grounds that severity would lose its impact over time, so requiring even tougher punishments until the point was reached where they became wholly disproportionate to the crime. This was the basis for his critique of capital punishment. He doubted that it would have much effect on the psychology of those inclined to murder, while in terms of dissuading others he considered execution to be transient in its impact. Long imprisonment would leave a more lasting impression. Contemporary research confirms this view. This issue remains extremely important, particularly in the United States, where deterrence is believed to be constantly tested in the claims surrounding the role of the death penalty in reducing the incidence of homicide. Those in favour of the death penalty do argue the deterrent effect, but not only the deterrent effect. Here, as in international affairs, a number of audiences are being addressed with the same policy. Proponents of capital punishment also view it in terms of retribution: a morality has to be upheld whatever the functional benefits. Faced with appalling crimes, many in the population demand vengeance. There is also the claim that executions at least ensure that murderers are never in a position to reoffend. Nonetheless, deterrence remains an important objective. Politicians who support the death penalty often seem more comfortable with deterrent than with retributive arguments, so that they can claim that even in taking lives they are saving lives. Opposition to the death penalty has a wide basis as well, including moral principles based on the sanctity of human life, but it also reflects doubts about deterrence.[2]

During the 1930s a famous study directed by Jack Gibbs concluded that capital punishment did not deter. This view was challenged in the 1970s by Isaac Ehrlich, who calculated that for each execution between 1933 and 1969 eight homicides had been prevented. Others have made similar claims.[3] Yet these results could not be reproduced, and later studies reverted to Gibbs's original view. For example, although there were a high number of executions in Texas between 1984 and 1997, the number appeared to be unrelated to murder rates in general. When Oklahoma returned to capital punishment in 1989 after a twenty-five-year moratorium, any expectation that there would be a reduction in the rates of murder and other forms of killing, for instance as the result of robberies or arguments, was not borne out. Indeed, there was a significant *increase* in stranger killings and non-felony stranger killings. The same result was found in Los Angeles after California returned to executions in 1992 after twenty-five years. In the eight months following the first execution there was a slight increase in criminal homicides. Studies tend to suggest that, in general, capital punishment accompanies higher rather than lower violent crime rates.[4] In 1995, 386 randomly selected police chiefs and county sheriffs in a telephone survey described the death penalty as the least favoured means of reducing violent crime. Most were concerned with tackling the conditions that encouraged crimes – drug abuse and unemployment. Then came the simplification of court rules, longer sentences, more police officers and reducing the number of guns. Two-thirds of the police chiefs considered the statement 'The death penalty significantly reduces the number of homicides' to be inaccurate. A former New York Police Chief wrote: 'Like the emperor's new clothes, the flimsy notion that the death penalty is an effective law enforcement tool is being exposed as mere political puffery.'[5]

Supporters of the death penalty do not accept these conclusions. They note that the problem with all studies of deterrence is that those who have been deterred from committing a crime do not show up in the statistics. Deterrence might also not work because of the half-heartedness of the policy, so that, in practice, executions are delayed and few are actually carried out. Juries become reluctant to convict if the guilty are to be executed: defence teams are more likely to submit pleas of insanity. The lack of certain and swift justice may undermine the effect. If, however, the empirical research is correct and the evidence does not support a deterrent effect, then some explanations are needed for why not. One possibility might be that those with murderous intent are insensitive to the value of all human life, including their own. More likely, many murders are crimes of passion, when the acts have been governed by fierce emotions or excessive drink rather than rational calculations of detection and punishment. Such murderers are of course also the most likely to get caught: those deliberately and coolly committing crimes do their best to avoid detection and may be less deterred by the prospect of apprehension. If they do recognize the risk, then the prospect of life imprisonment may well be as much of a deterrent as the death penalty.

Even with non-capital punishments, such as long sentences, the deterrent impact may be affected by the requirement that it meets other criteria. It is supposed to incapacitate people who would otherwise be a danger to the community, and also be retributive, in reinforcing the public's sense of outrage. There is a tension between these measures, which should have the long-term effect of reinforcing communal notions of morality and acceptable behaviour, and attempts to draw wrongdoers back into the community through programmes aimed at providing them with work and social skills. The evidence suggests that long custodial sentences tend to reinforce criminal norms and skills and encourage recidivism, so this is not a good means of cutting future crime.

Nonetheless, there is substantial evidence that in many areas of crime sentencing creates a deterrent effect. A recent University of Cambridge survey concluded:

> For at least some classes of potential offenders, their percep-
> tions of the risks of being apprehended and punished (when
> they are aware of such risks) affect their reported choices of
> whether to offend. These studies thus help confirm that
> known penal threats can have a deterrent effect. However,
> the studies with the least methodological problems (those
> based on scenarios of offending) are mostly concerned with
> informal sanctions; and, to the extent they address criminal-
> justice responses at all, deal with 'certainty' variables such as
> perceived likelihood of prosecution. They thus do not shed
> much light on questions of severity effects.

Changing the marginal severity of punishments therefore appears to have far less effect than increasing the certainty that crime will result in some punishment. One important reason why changes in severity may have little impact is that actual sentencing practice is not well known, and there is often substantial public underestimation of how tough punishments can be. As the Cambridge study observed, 'potential offenders cannot be deterred by sentencing changes of which they are unaware'. The announcement of a change may have less effect than its actual implementation being communicated back through the social networks of offenders – but this may not help with potential offenders.[6]

One might add that those offenders influenced by alcohol or drugs, responsible for a substantial proportion of violent crime, may have rendered themselves incapable of an informed risk calculus. At the same time, individuals who are more socialized, with strong ties of family and community, are likely to be more amenable to deterrence. This is an important conclusion and is relevant for the development of norms-based deterrence.

The criminological literature also has its own distinction between general and immediate (or specific) deterrence, and while the role of the death penalty in specific deterrence may appear to have the greatest resonance for strategic debates, the issues raised by general deterrence may be more valid. General deterrence involves all the social references, from displayed warnings to highly publicized crack-downs that infuse certain types of activity with a sense of deviancy, danger and punishment. It is therefore about a process of building up norms, to be internalized by individuals, which leads them away from even thinking about certain forms of anti-social activity. This describes what I have referred to as internalized deterrence. The censure of the courts and the sense of stigma conveyed by third parties should be manifest in the shame felt by the offender. What starts with a fear of punishment may conclude with a changed moral outlook. Research in a number of areas suggests that the extra-legal consequences of crime are at least as great a deterrent as the legal consequences. Indeed, the legal consequences may be felt through their effect on the extra-legal – the 'stigma from arrest'.[7] The corollary of this is that the more common a crime becomes, the less of a stigma is the ensuing punishment. With some offences, such as taking marijuana, an effective counter-norm may develop so that a substantial section of the community fails to recognize that there is a crime. Alternatively, a criminal sub-culture may develop which rejects the norms of the rest of society. Even the prospect of punishment itself may be seen as unthreatening. Time in jail may be seen as quite normal among certain social groups – and even as a badge of honour.

A good example of how norms can work positively comes with the deterrence of drunken driving. In such cases the offenders may not consider themselves to be naturally delinquent or irrational. Because of the danger they pose to others when under the influence of alcohol, deterrence is critical. As so many journeys are taken every day, many with drunks at the wheel, catching all offenders would be impossible. Excessive alcohol is often only detected as a result of testing, while routine patrols and cameras help spot erratic driving or speeding, even before an accident. Research on this issue suggests that successful deterrence depends on:

- the impression conveyed that arrest is at least a serious possibly;
- successful prosecutions: these require there to be clear standards of intoxication, and the reliable use of the breathalyser or blood tests to measure these;
- an acceptable level of alcohol: most drivers have a view of recklessness (somewhat over their levels) and if the standards are too excessive, they will rebel against the laws – or at least against disproportionate sentences;
- effective publicity, such as special campaigns and patrols and some highly publicized arrests;
- evidence that significant reductions in offences and accidents can result.

When the sentences are too severe, judges and juries are often reluctant to apply them, so the net effect is to undermine them. The world's first drinking and driving laws, enacted in Norway in 1936 and in Sweden in 1941, often led to imprisonment. In 1975 it was concluded that this was having no effect on the incidence of fatal crashes, which led to a reorientation of sentencing to emphasize the certainty of punishment over the severity of punishment. All evidence now suggests that programmes based on high visibility and rigorous enforcement that can be sustained over a long period – that is, punishments which bother potential offenders without appearing unfair – are more effective. So here we can see a norm being created through positive acts of persuasion, so that drinking and driving appears as a truly anti-social act and there is peer pressure to desist, as well as well-judged punishments.

More specific deterrence has to work on individual decision-making, in circumstances where it must be assumed that the normative element, so important to general deterrence, barely applies and so the prospect of arrest and tough punishment becomes much more important. Yet punishment may mean little when few are arrested and effectively prosecuted. If the punishment rates are judged to be too severe, then juries may be more inclined to give defendants the benefit of the doubt. Alternatively, if apprehension rates are low and police resources become stretched, then a vicious cycle may come into play and certain crimes appear to carry a minimal risk to the offender. So the strictly utilitarian view of deterrence has been qualified over time by an awareness of the importance of emotions and values. Indeed, as noted earlier, the case for the death penalty depends as much on reinforcing morality as on deterrence. The severity of the crime is underlined by the severity of the punishment, even though this may undermine the efficiency of deterrence by making punishment less certain.

Not surprisingly, deterrence works best when the targets are able to act rationally, and when the deterrer and the deterred are working within a sufficiently shared normative framework that it is possible to inculcate a sense of appropriate behaviour in defined situations that can be reinforced by a combination of social pressures and a sense of fair and effective punishment. Out of this comes a view that criminal deterrence might work through the complex interaction between a government seeking to encourage the idea that certain behaviour is anti-social and elements in society that are sympathetic to this idea. Those otherwise inclined to act improperly are therefore deterred not only by the prospect of punishment, but also the disapproval of their friends and neighbours when their crime becomes known. The deterrent effect becomes less necessary as they come to share this definition of what is anti-social. If they do not share this definition, of course, then deterrence may cease to function, for then they will feel no shame, disregard any stigma and accept no censure.

Norms in International Relations

Criminological studies of deterrence are better founded than those coming from international relations because they have far superior data sets. They draw upon numerous and comparable cases, although there are still methodological problems in assessing inaction, in controlling for all the relevant variables, and in knowing whether experiments (often involving handy groups of students) designed to test popular attitudes towards crime will provide guides to actual behaviour. There are other grounds for caution in arguing that these findings are directly relevant to the study of international relations. With crime, the test of deterrence lies in reducing the incidence of a particular sort of offence, but there can be no expectation of its total eradication. Deterrence failures have to be assessed in the aggregate rather than the specific. In international relations, by contrast, there is no accepted and monitored rate of outrageous international behaviour to check. A single severe incident can have substantial repercussions yet be quite unique. Most importantly, there is no equivalent in the international system of the central authority within states that presides over the criminal justice system and upon which basic deterrence depends.

There are, however, ways of talking about the international system that play down its anarchic character and consider patterns of behaviour that might be influenced by the views of that amorphous body known as the 'international community'. This approach is consistent with that normally attributed to the 'English School' in international relations, which takes as its starting point classical realism, but assumes that the complex interaction among states both depends upon and helps to generate shared values, and produces something which can be described as an international society.[8] This framework lends itself to the consideration of the development of norms, because that is exactly the process that helps bind the society of states together. In this context, one interesting question becomes whether certain norms – such as non-aggression – can be upheld without forms of collective enforcement, or whether other related norms, judged crucial in the past, can at some point become dysfunctional. For example, the principle of non-interference in another state's internal affairs was challenged as the internal affairs of weak states became regular sources of international turbulence. There is a developing literature of international relations theory, known as constructivism, which is interested in how actors constitute themselves, and how norms become insinuated into the attitudes and behaviour of actors on the international stage.[9] This has encouraged a growing focus on the role of norms, defined by Katzenstein as 'the standard of appropriate behaviour for actors with a given identity'.[10] They can both set limits on and encourage distinctive types of behaviour (constraining and enabling) and can also be constitutive in shaping how actors think about themselves. They are bound up with notions of legitimacy, a key ingredient for any action that depends on the support and approbation of others, and which can be found at an intersection close to legality, morality and social acceptability. There is therefore a potentially supportive environment for making an assessment of whether there are circumstances in which the processes of censure, shame and stigma that work at the national level might also work at the international level.

This constructivist turn, which draws on mainstream sociology, can encourage the view that ideas are drivers in themselves. Critics, often with good reason, have linked it to traditional forms of idealism which sought to promote good international behaviour by institutionalizing it. Here the stress was on the development of international law and its enforcement through international organizations, to match the maintenance of law and order in domestic settings. The key norms of state practice, such as non-aggression and non-interference in internal affairs, have gained strength through their appearance in authoritative documents such as the UN Charter and their regular repetition by international jurists and political leaders. When Iraq invaded Kuwait in 1990, for example, it was widely asserted (for example by British Prime Minister Margaret Thatcher) that if such behaviour were allowed to flourish, the only law in place would be that of the jungle. Constructivists take this view further by looking at types of behaviour that may or may not be proscribed by international treaty but which are nonetheless ruled out by states that might otherwise have been expected to see an advantage.

The origin of the word 'taboo' comes from Polynesia and refers to local customs that must be respected. These proscribe behaviour to an extent that it is moved beyond serious consideration, such as cannibalism in Western societies. Even raising the issue becomes daring and excites disapproval. This does not mean that over time certain proscriptions cannot come to be lifted, such as open homosexuality, or cannot vary from one society to another, as with monogamy. Schelling, the greatest of the deductive theorists, in part because he never allowed himself to be imprisoned by methodology, explored the 'taboo' in connection with nuclear weapons. This taboo was first identified by Eisenhower's Secretary of State John Foster Dulles, who thought it deplorable, and some in the Eisenhower Administration considered that it would be helpful to find some occasion to use the weapons just to break the taboo. No occasion was found and the weapons remained under this 'curse', despite attempts to obscure the distinction between them and conventional weapons, because of their uniquely destructive quality. Schelling considers this an asset.[11] Price and Tannenwald have also examined the taboos against chemical and nuclear use.[12] It is important to their argument that even when there might have been instrumental reasons for employment – for example, tactical nuclear weapons to regain the initiative during the Vietnam War – this appeared to be so odious that the option was rejected. Chemical weapons had begun to trigger revulsion during the First World War: hence their non-use (at least in Europe) during the Second. Desch, as part of his critique of this type of argument, suggests that a better explanation lies in the limited military utility of the weapons and the risks of retaliation, that is deterrence, as much as any odium. When the risk of retaliation was slight, a number of countries had few compunctions about using chemical weapons.[13] Even so, it is clear that there are political costs attached to the use of such weapons, even on a small scale. The very distinction between 'weapons of mass destruction' and 'conventional weapons' indicates that extraordinary justifications might be required. Governments would rather not pay these costs even though, in desperate circumstances, they might not be prohibitive.

It may be the case that the focus on how these norms are created and sustained fits in with a traditional idealist agenda, but there is no reason why this approach need ignore the factors of power and interest that preoccupy realists. Case studies of the development of norms confirm that those that prosper are likely to be sponsored by powerful interests, and also that they are by no means always wholesome. Jenkins demonstrates how the concept of terrorism has been 'shaped by social and political processes, by bureaucratic needs and media structures'. This has important consequences: some groups are demonized while others get a free pass for similar acts.[14] Ward Thomas has researched the reasons for the development of the norm against assassinating foreign leaders (not an obvious conclusion of moral reasoning given that their survival may condemn many more to death). He shows how it came about through the interaction between emerging moral principles and structural influences, including the interests of powerful actors in the international system. Once established,

> the norm itself served a legitimizing function, reinforcing institutional changes by providing them with a normative foundation based on natural law principles of justice and honor. The norm addressed new political concerns, connect-

ing moral judgements to emerging interests in a way that they had not been previously.[15]

So norms gain strength by being connected to powerful interests. Equally, if these interests decline, or moral discourse suggests a change, then norms can go into decline.

Bad norms can also gain in social acceptability, at least in a particular locality. Although these have not been much studied,[16] the situation is starting to be rectified. Fujii, for example, has studied the development of the 'genocidal' norm in Rwanda that had such devastating consequences in 1994. She draws attention to:

> [the] use of media to make genocide everyday 'talk' and the use of myths to interpret the significance and meaning of current crises and to prescribe clear solutions to the dangers these crises posed. By skillfully exploiting the resources of the past and the opportunities of the present, the *génocidaires* were able to construct a world where genocidal thinking was the norm, and to make that world the only consequential reality for victim and killer alike.[17]

Power counts if norms are to be established. The question then becomes whether threats of force can play any role in the development of norms. At first glance this seems unlikely. The point about norms is that they have been internalized so that they are followed because they seem right rather than through the threat of punishment. Florini, for example, takes on Axelrod's view that the 'extent to which a given type of action is a norm depends on just how often the action is taken and just how often someone is punished for not taking it', by arguing that this pays insufficient regard to the extent to which individuals incorporate norms into their own belief systems without punishment being threatened.[18] It is the legitimacy of the norms rather than the threat of punishment that is the key. In discussing this, Fujii correctly notes that while 'norms may not derive their legitimacy from enforcement, they may nonetheless benefit from it'. Norms are not necessarily self-reinforcing. Interestingly in the light of our earlier discussion of the criminological literature, she gives as an example upholding a speed limit for drivers.[19]

It has long been understood by political leaders that the best source of power is that which refreshes itself and does not have to be reinforced by regular acts of brute force. If the source is accepted as a legitimate authority, then it is possible to encourage people to take their cues on the attitudes to adopt and appropriate forms of behaviour. Such cues do not only come from governments or international organizations, such as the UN, but also from the church or even academic 'experts'. Some non-governmental organizations, while lobbying for a particular point of view, acquire sufficient authority to challenge official views, for example on environmental matters. Constructivist writers speak of 'norm entrepreneurs', competing to establish norms, having to find forms of words to demonstrate that their norm fits in with those already embedded and can work to the greater good, while at the same time disparaging alternative norms that would undermine their own. This reflects one aspect of everyday political life. The promotion of norms is core government business, and when a government is unable to do this, then its authority is under severe challenge and it is on the road to having to rely on brute force. Governments have an advantage because of their capacity to enforce, but when their dominant ideas have become so contested that they no longer gain assent, and they still try to impose them, then the result may be a counter-reaction, and even forceful challenges to their authority. The importance of the quality of the appeals made to the population is evident in theories on countering guerrilla warfare and terrorism that emphasize the importance of winning over the 'hearts and minds' of the population, rather than just searching for and then destroying the enemy.

Can we think of international affairs in the same way? Even when nations feel at their most threatened, the values they claim to live by remain important, providing the motivation for the continuing struggle. When the struggle is less desperate, legitimacy is certainly an issue in the conduct of their foreign policy, especially when it comes to the use of force. It has been evident in recent disputes that states engaged in coercive practices consider their position to be strengthened if they can point to international agreements or, better still, specific undertakings that embody the norms that their targets are deemed to have violated.[20] *Raison d'état* no longer suffices for their own populations, while shared values and concerns are the basis for gaining support in international organizations or in forming coalitions and alliances. It is possible to dismiss alternative sources of international authority, such as the United Nations or the International Committee of the Red Cross, but that carries a cost, and so long as costs are involved and calculations have to be made about what costs are acceptable in relation to possible gains, then deterrence of some sort is in play.

Changes in the international situation have an effect on the normative as well as the power structure within which foreign policy is conducted. The continuing relevance of deterrence became an issue not only because of the dramatic changes that took place in international relations after the late 1980s. By this time, immediate deterrence already seemed a thing of the past and general deterrence was barely pertinent. Then the security problem that had been dominant for more than four decades evaporated along with European communism, the Warsaw Pact and, at the end of 1991, the Soviet Union itself. The problems then faced by the successor regimes made it even harder to take seriously scenarios of a resurgent threat from the East. In this context, at least in NATO, it was difficult to identify anything other than a marginal role for nuclear threats, both received and delivered. Military establishments began to gear themselves up in readiness for a series of more limited wars and 'operations other than war'. From a situation in which the potential enemy was known and the likely arenas of conflict readily identified, there was a move to one in which everything appeared as uncertain and ambiguous. If there was still a requirement for deterrence, it was for something specific to a particular crisis and a particular capability (such as chemical weapons) at a particular time. This pointed back to the original concept of an occasional stratagem rather than a constant, all-purpose stance.

Beyond Bipolarity

Deterrence theory during the cold war had reflected an underlying symmetry in military capabilities. An unwillingness to confront the ideological challenge presented by communism could result in the transformation of the political life and socio-economic organization of whole continents; a false step in the other direction and civilization itself might be swept away. Not surprisingly, the corresponding conceptual framework that emerged out of academic and policy debates was geared towards steering a middle course between these two potential catastrophes. A conflict that could not be securely resolved either through diplomacy or war required strategies that demonstrated determination but that were, at the same time, infused with caution and restraint: containment, stability, crisis management, détente, arms control and deterrence. The preferred alternative to escalation was to seek a common intent to avoid fighting, represented by the strategic paraphernalia of hot lines, confidence-building measures, and summits. Such strategies were reinforced by principles of international law, which stressed non-interference in internal affairs and the use of military action strictly for the purpose of self-defence. US military deployments were as important in terms of their capacity to reassure allies about American commitment as in their relevance to hypothetical scenarios in which the credibility of threats might be challenged. Deterrence therefore gained prominence as a representative of a set of related concepts, all reflecting the situational constraints of the time.

Over this period the international system was described as being 'bipolar'. The two poles were the superpowers to which all other states were obliged to relate for security purposes. Because neither pole could defeat the other, their antagonism could not be resolved and so acquired a sense of permanence. During the 1950s and 1960s there were attempts by the superpowers to apply it elsewhere by engaging in competitive alliance formation around the world. By and large, these imitation alliances withered and died, or else had such a flimsy base as to be meaningless. Later, in the name of anti-communism or anti-imperialism, the United States and the Soviet Union also found themselves acquiring clients with minimal interest in either cause but a considerable stake in surviving a civil war or protecting themselves from traditional rivals in their locality.

In practice, outside Europe, bipolarity's influence had long been declining. This was the result of the inexorable processes of decolonization. The 1950s saw the first celebration of 'non-alignment' as an explicit attempt to escape from the logic of bipolarity. In the 1960s more regimes were released from colonization and, with others, sought to assert their independence from 'imperialism'. During that decade China's break with the Soviet Union encouraged thoughts of a 'tripolar' world. By the 1970s this trend had been consolidated and was reflected in such developments as the rise of OPEC and the presumption that the East–West confrontation was being superseded by one based on the even greater geographical simplification of 'North–South'. Because demarcation lines in the third world were not so clearly set, ideological loyalties were fickle and military balances were ambiguous, the major powers found themselves being drawn into messy regional conflicts in the mistaken belief that this was part of some grand strategic game. Specialists on the various regions warned of the limits of the East–West, bipolar model as an interpretative device, and gradually the truth of this became apparent.

The superpowers learned the hard way about the dangers of involvement in particular regional conflicts, where each believed it must block a strategic advance by its adversary. In a misguided attempt to take advantage of American hesitation following the Vietnam disaster, the Soviet Union supported a series of notionally left-wing regimes, none of which was able to assert its authority effectively and most of which were a drain on Soviet resources. The American reluctance to accept new military commitments in the third world after Vietnam was palpable and quite natural. The Nixon doctrine of 1969 suggested that in the future the United States would only help friendly states which helped themselves. America's wretched experience does not appear to have had much impact on Soviet expectations, perhaps on the comfortable ideological presumption that they truly were working with the progressive forces of history. This culminated in the Afghanistan intervention, which persuaded Moscow thereafter to steer clear of further such commitments. Although the introduction of superpower rivalry into regional conflicts was seen to carry the risk of escalation to something much worse, in practice growing superpower caution meant that this risk declined.

In Europe, bipolarity involved a military equilibrium between two opposed forms of social-economic-political organization, which was eventually upset as a result of the dynamics of internal change in the communist bloc. A shared fear of war encouraged toleration of an inconclusive standoff as opposed to high-risk attempts to resolve the fundamental ideological conflict, but it could do nothing about the internal threats to the Soviet state. A prudent, mutual accommodation between the superpowers was by no means the same as a freezing of the status quo. Although communism's European collapse appeared as a sharp discontinuity, it could also be presented as the culmination of the decolonization process. Fifteen years after the last Western empire – the Portuguese – collapsed, the post-1945 Soviet acquisitions were liberated, with the finale coming in an implosion of the old Russian Empire. Fragmentation occurred in the Soviet Union and other post-communist states, most painfully in Yugoslavia, but also in Czechoslovakia.

From an oasis of stability in an unstable world, Europe suddenly appeared as among the most turbulent of continents. Old states fell apart and new ones were created, all sharing economic fragility but otherwise varying greatly in culture, tradition and potential international weight. There was even talk of isolated famine and mass migration. In some areas violence became endemic and routine. A long-locked cupboard, packed full of old worn ideologies and prejudices, suddenly burst open. In this way problems that once seemed quintessentially 'third world' became common in Europe. Meanwhile, the former third world was also influenced by these developments. States that were once bound together by a shared anti-colonial impulse now found other issues more salient. There did not seem to be much point in talking about the third world; not only did it contain so many disparate and often conflictual elements, but also the second world had collapsed. Of the old geopolitical labels, only the 'West' seemed to have any relevance, because the grouping to which it referred still cohered and a high value was placed on close cooperation among its members.

Bipolarity was an obvious victim of changed circumstances, but so also was the representation of the international system upon which it was based – that of a magnetic field governing the political behaviour of the individual state units. With bipolarity, all states were drawn to one of two poles, acknowledging that the level of attraction was weak in a number of cases and that other states, through non-alignment, sought to resist the pulls. Its continuing influence was suggested by the proclamation of a 'unipolar' world led by the United States. The fact that a 'unipolar' world was almost immediately taken seriously was an interesting commentary on fashions in punditry, given that 'declinism' was in vogue barely two years earlier, and that other analysts had assumed not that bipolarity would shrink into unipolarity, but that it would grow into multipolarity with new centres of power. In practice, the United States moved even beyond superpower status in military terms – to a 'super-duper-power' or 'hyperpower'. It was also, at least during the 1990s, the most dynamic force in the international economy. In raw military power the Americans were moving into a class of their own, to the point where they no longer needed allied contributions to their military operations to fill gaps in their own provision.

Interests, Vital and Otherwise

Western states, at least, seemed to have few vital interests at stake in the many conflicts that still raged around the world. Their now ascendant economic and social systems had brought them prosperity and victory, yet this very success meant that they had become a force for change rather than a means of resisting change. With liberal issues of human rights and environmentalism moving up the agenda, demands began to be put on other countries that were seen to fall far short of Western standards. Interests were identified in establishing and enforcing rules for a more civilized international system, including general respect for minorities and open economic practices. Here, norms and interests came together, as a view developed of the sort of international system with which the Western states would feel most at ease, sparing them from the aftershocks of turbulence elsewhere and allowing them to prosper in safety. In the ideal system they would not only have the most power but also others would adopt them as models, embracing their values and modes of political and economic organization. Other countries, claiming as great an interest in the welfare of their citizens and economic growth, were wary of attempts to generalize from a particular culture and to assert the superiority of a Western way of life. Hence, for example, the claims made on behalf of 'Asian values'. As serious was the question of what Western states intended to do on behalf of norms that were being violated. It was one thing to point out that countries which rejected Western norms fared badly and quite another to intervene when the conditions within those countries became dire.

Well before the end of the cold war, a series of tensions and conflicts in Africa, Asia and the Middle East, which occasionally erupted violently and viciously, increasingly began to develop dynamics all of their own. By the early 1990s these had extended into post-communist Europe. These conflicts usually took the form of civil war and saw an intermingling of the civilian and military spheres, with the fighting often conducted by militias and against local people. For Western countries, the issue was no longer one of enforcing demands but of whether sufficient interests were at stake for any demands to be made in the first place. Interests had become matters of choice, to be shaped through an appreciation of the nature of the challenge faced and the cost of meeting it. With no overriding strategic imperatives, questions of interest remained vague until they were pushed to the fore by a crisis. Interests had become less fixed and challenges more unpredictable. Neo-realists assumed that when hard interests and norms conflict, then the former must win, but when the interests become softer, and start to include views about the proper organization of the international system and approved codes of behaviour, then there is much more for the 'norm entrepeneurs' to play for. Until July 1990 there was no particular reason to care about Kuwait, and in 1992 the future condition of Bosnia appeared to be of scant consequence to the United States. The effects of other peoples' conflicts might be felt, for example with people seeking asylum or the knock-on effects of economic chaos, but these interests would not in themselves be sufficient to warrant any intervention. Yet in the face of compelling media images of human suffering it was also hard to make a case for passivity. If Western norms meant anything, they had to be applied internationally as well as nationally. Whether or not there was a hard material interest at stake in these conflicts, they posed a direct challenge to values that were supposedly cherished. The question then became one of the costs might need to be incurred to uphold these values.

Prior to a crisis, there was bound to be a reluctance to make promises that might prove difficult to keep. Western states became anxious about expectations that they would be willing and able to sort out every local conflict, which could result in a series of inconclusive and domestically unpopular entanglements. So international action was bound to become more discretionary, depending on how serious a situation appeared, as well as the reactions of other states that might be prepared to support action and of those who might take exception, the prospects for diplomacy and the feasibility of military options, and the long-term consequences of getting involved in other peoples' problems. Whether or not to intervene in particular conflicts – in Somalia but not in Rwanda, tentatively in Bosnia but assertively in Kosovo – was a matter of choice for those few powers with an expeditionary capability, mainly the United States, the United Kingdom and France.

The attacks of 9/11 jolted the American debate back to fundamental questions of national security. Whether this return is permanent will depend on whether 9/11 turns out to have been a one-off or a super-terrorist trend, and also whether it encourages the view that third world turmoil has to be addressed lest it become a breeding ground for future super-terrorists. At a time when the international hierarchy of power appeared to have reached a stark and singular clarity, the system still had a capacity to surprise and alarm. Furthermore, while these attacks represented a deliberate act of aggression, albeit mounted by a non-state group, they were linked to a range of conflicts of considerable complexity and did not present themselves in an unambiguous form. This was normal for challenges emerging out of remote conflict, gradually as local situations deteriorated and the levels of violence grew, rather than as a result of a deliberate offensive move by one side. There was not one fateful calculation that could be influenced by considerations of how the major powers might respond. Furthermore, even if and when such deliberations did take place and consideration was given to the involvement of outside powers, it would be hard to be sure exactly what form any external involvement might take. There could be no certainty in the response of others.

After 9/11, US strategy became more urgent and less relaxed. While the source of the threat and the means of delivery was novel, it also fitted in with long-established American fears of surprise attacks in the form of a bolt from the skies. This was a function of geography and history, of Pearl Harbor and the years when the Soviet Union appeared

to be forging ahead with intercontinental missile deployments. The attacks against New York and Washington were
traumatic but hardly decisive. It was possible to deal with the
perpetrators in an effort to reduce the possibilities that such
a blow would ever be struck again. Yet the Americans were
left feeling extraordinarily vulnerable. Although a hyperpower without a military peer among states, the USA turned
out to be unexpectedly vulnerable to a murky underworld
of gangsters and terrorists who might just acquire devastating instruments either by complicity from rogue states or by
capitalizing on the anarchy of weak states.

As far as the United States was concerned, two events – the collapse of Soviet power (and Russia's new friendship with the United States) followed by the apparent rise of super-terrorism – together suggested that deterrence was no longer relevant as a strategy. Instead, 'pre-emption' was offered as a more appropriate alternative. This principle – that it is better to deal with threats before they are realized – was spelled out in the September 2002 National Security Strategy (NSS) document. The principle, as the President put it, drew on every politician's nightmare: 'History will judge harshly those who saw this coming danger but failed to act.' The possibility that rogue elements within the international system might acquire weapons of mass destruction and use them was rated to be even more menacing than the cold war.

What really made the difference, according to the new policy, were the 'nature and motivations of these new adversaries, their determination to obtain destructive powers hitherto available only to the world's strongest states, and the greater likelihood that they will use weapons of mass destruction against us.' Before, there was a 'status quo, risk-averse adversary' against whom deterrence might work, and weapons of mass destruction were considered to be only 'of last resort'. An enemy with martyrs for foot-soldiers, weapons of mass destruction as firepower and 'wanton destruction and the targeting of innocents' as a core objective could not be handled by traditional means. This did not mean, however, that pre-emption would serve any better as a concept.

Prevention and Pre-emption

The distinction between coercive and controlling strategies helps illuminate the debate between deterrence and pre-emption. Deterrence is coercive because A relies on influencing B's decisions rather than eliminating B's capacity for decision. Let us suppose that instead of A being so confident in its strength and determination to defend its vital interests that it is sure it deters B, A sees instead that B is getting stronger. In time, it could advance and overwhelm resistance or blunt the impact of retaliation. Aware of this possibility, A may decide to act to prevent B from reaching this position. This would qualify as a *preventive war* if it had at least one of two potential objectives. The first, at a minimum, would be to disarm B to keep it unambiguously militarily inferior. The second would be to change the political character of B's state so that, even if allowed to rearm, it would no longer pose a threat. The latter, more ambitious, objective would be more militarily demanding, but disarmament without regime change would mean that an embittered victim would just rearm with greater vigour. The first objective is controlling because it denies B a type of decision; the second because it changes the whole character of B as a decision-maker. So prevention exploits existing strategic advantages by depriving another state of the capability to pose a threat and/or eliminating the state's motivation to pose a threat through regime change. Prevention provides a means of confronting factors that are likely to contribute to the development of a threat before it has had a chance to become imminent.

Should A decide not to instigate a preventive war, and B acquires that extra strength, then, eventually, B may come to feel that it has acquired the upper hand and can safely take the initiative against A. At this point, A may come to regret its past restraint and decide that there is no more time to lose. A pre-emptive war takes place at some point between the moment when an enemy decides to attack – or more precisely, is perceived to be about to attack – and the attack is actually launched. This is what the international lawyers call 'anticipatory self-defence'. For A, challenges lie in both the quality of the evidence of imminent attack by B and the ability of its forces to disrupt the attack at this stage. If not disrupted effectively, then A's attack is bound to prompt a response from B that otherwise might have been avoided. After all, a favourable balance of power is not the only factor that influences an actor's decision to go to war, and there might have been good reason for B to have eschewed taking advantage of its new military superiority or at least waiting until there was a genuine cause to use it. Thus pre-emption, especially if prompted by a worst-case assumption about what an opponent just might be planning, could well start a war when there might not have been one otherwise. A will hope that by taking the initiative the balance of power will have been reset in its favour, whether or not the war continues. So pre-emption is a controlling strategy to the extent that it seeks to remove or reduce the enemy's capacity to control.

Prevention is cold-blooded: it intends to deal with a problem before it becomes a crisis, while pre-emption is a more desperate strategy employed in the heat of crisis. Prevention can be seen as pre-emption in slow motion, more anticipatory or forward thinking, perhaps even looking beyond the target's current intentions to those that might be acquired along with greatly enhanced capabilities. There is, in addition, another important difference.[1] With prevention, A has great advantages in deciding when to attack and doing so while B remains inferior. It should be possible to find an optimum moment when B is quite unprepared and not at all alert. And even if B can fully appreciate what A is planning, it might still be helpless. With pre-emption, on the other hand, B may no longer be inferior or unprepared, causing the possibility that A, even if taking only precautionary moves to prepare a pre-emptive contingency, might be noticed and provoke B's strike. Pre-emption requires, at the very least, that A believes it is more likely to win any war that it initiates. An attack that does not cripple the enemy will only succeed if good use can be made politically, as well as militarily, of the extra time gained as the enemy recovers.

Pre-emption is directed specifically at the enemy's most dangerous capabilities and thus sets for itself a very serious but unambiguous test. If B's targeted capability escapes largely unscathed, then it is likely to be used at once. If the concern was serious enough to warrant the attack, then the military consequences of failure must be very severe. With prevention, by contrast, the military test is bound to be milder, because of B's inferiority. As with pre-emptive action, and whatever the enemy's actual intentions, it will usher in an irreversible move from peace to war, but one in which victory should be assured. On the other hand, the political test will be much more severe, with the threat more distant and open to subjective interpretation. The superior power can expect to be accused of bullying, acting prematurely, perhaps on no more than a hunch. To the extent that A does not care about international opinion, this may not matter, but without a compelling cause preventive war can soon look like any other sort of aggressive war and cause a reaction else-where, from diplomatic isolation to the development of alliances among potential victims.

How did this work during the cold war? The possibility of preventive war was discussed up to the mid-1950s in Washington at a time when the USA had at first a nuclear monopoly and then clear superiority but could see that the Soviet Union was engaged in an energetic effort to catch up. The discussions were at times serious, especially when it became evident during the first year of the Eisenhower Administration that Moscow was close to a thermonuclear capability. In the end, such a move was rejected as being too risky and of doubtful legality, especially from a country still smarting as a result of the surprise Japanese attack of

7 December 1941. Preventive war was also discussed in relation to China, the rising and revolutionary power of the 1960s. President Kennedy mused about how he would like to prevent it from becoming a nuclear power, but as it approached an operational capability it was the Soviet Union that seemed to look upon the prospect with the most grave forebodings. In 1969 Moscow went so far as to hint that a strike was being planned against Chinese nuclear assets, to the point where the United States felt obliged to make it known that it could not support such a move.

When it decided that the risks of preventive war were too great, the United States had no choice but to allow the Soviet Union to acquire extra nuclear strength. By October 1957 the launch of Sputnik, the world's first artificial earth satellite, confirmed a capacity to send intercontinental ballistic missiles (ICBMs) to attack the continental United States. Concern grew that Moscow might feel that it enjoyed the upper hand and could aggress with impunity. The only apparent way to win a nuclear war was to eliminate the enemy's nuclear capability before it could be used. The trouble with this model where nuclear weapons were concerned was that if only a small part of the targeted assets survived and could be launched in retaliation, the consequences could be catastrophic. The nuclear arsenals became so big and the proportions needed to inflict terrible damage so slight that pre-emption simply risked bringing about that which it was supposed to prevent.

Pre-emption reflects the belief that the first action will be crucial, and that one dare not be the victim. This was captured by the notions of first and second strike. A *first-strike* capability would involve disarming the enemy in a surprise, pre-emptive attack, destroying as much as possible of his means of retaliation on the ground and intercepting any bombers or missiles that escaped before they reached their targets. If such an attack could be absorbed and then followed by a retaliation that would avoid overwhelming enemy defences, that would be a *second-strike* capability. In the event, both the United States and the Soviet Union acquired systems that could withstand attacks or remain hidden, while missile defences always seemed porous.

Norms, Pre-emption and International Law

This issue provides an interesting example of how norms about acceptable international behaviour develop and change. Prevention is legally dubious because it can appear simply as an act of aggression. Pre-emption deals with the threat just as it is about to be realized and so can be justified as an act of self-defence, dealing with the threat before the enemy is able to make resistance impossible. This legal justification, in the form of 'anticipatory self-defence', tends to be framed in terms of criteria set down by the then US Secretary of State Daniel Webster in 1842. In 1837 a steamship, *Caroline*, was attacked in American waters and then dispatched, ablaze, over the Niagara Falls by British forces to prevent its use to supply rebels in Canada. The controversy was settled through an exchange of diplomatic notes, in which Webster asserted that any claim of self-defence had to be shown to be 'instant, overwhelming, leaving no choice of means, and no moment for deliberation'. Furthermore, the measures taken should be proportionate, involving 'nothing unreasonable or excessive; since the act, justified by the necessity of self-defense, must be limited by that necessity and kept clearly within it'.

Although regularly cited as the foundation of international law in this area, it is by no means clear that this remains a particularly good guide in contemporary conditions, other than the requirement that if you are going to attack another country you should have a good reason for doing so and few reasons are more compelling than credible evidence that restraint is apt to be exploited. The rules that might guide you when an armed burglar is detected stumbling around your room may not be so helpful when dealing with a state with an evident intent to do you harm at some indeterminate time in the future. Furthermore, whether means are 'unreasonable or excessive' tends to be a matter of dispute. Few want to fight their battles with a minimum margin of error, and at times overwhelming force is the best means of avoiding excessive casualties and hardship. Anticipatory self-defence is still said to require that the threat be 'imminent', but this test cannot be easily judged over a set period of time. In practice, at issue is whether it is a threat that, if left alone, will soon reach a point where the risk is that any reactive defence will fail, or only succeed with exceptional effort. The USA no longer adopts Webster's formulation, preferring instead one associated with a former Secretary of War, Elihu Root, who noted in 1914, 'the right of every sovereign state to protect itself by preventing a condition of affairs in which it will be too late to protect itself'.

If the existence of the threat is largely speculative, but a country is invaded nonetheless 'just in case', then that might be deemed to be tantamount to aggression. The only potentially legitimate body that might decide this, however, is the UN Security Council, and its impartiality can never be beyond question. When it can agree on a threat to international peace and security, it can create international law or condemn breaches, but as often as not it cannot agree for reasons of political differences rather than legal interpretations. When Israel acted against what it believed to be a gathering Arab threat in June 1967 by striking the Egyptian Air Force, which did not stop the Egyptians (and the Jordanians and Syrians) fighting but guaranteed their defeat, the UN Security Council did not condemn this. The United States took the view that the Arab countries had asked for trouble by making war-like noises and preparations for some weeks, thereby heightening Israel's sense of insecurity. It may be, as historians now judge, that they had never expected to be taken that seriously, but Israel could not be sure of that.

By contrast, Israel's 1981 strike, when sixteen aircraft destroyed Iraq's Osirak reactor, was condemned (in Resolution 487) on the grounds that this time there was no imminent threat to Israel. On the other hand, no sanctions were imposed on Israel and in private there was some satisfaction that Iraq's nuclear programme had been set back. Iraqi claims of peaceful intent with Osirak were clearly false, and if the attack had been delayed until the reactor became more threatening, in terms of producing fissile material, it would have been too dangerous to bomb. The facility had been bombed but barely damaged by Iran the previous year. Tellingly, it has been reported that after the Iranian attack, Iraq issued a statement to the effect that the Iranian people should not fear the Iraqi nuclear reactor 'which is not intended to be used against Iran, but against the Zionist entity'.[2] In retrospect, given what later became known about Iraqi intentions, the action looked even better, although there is an argument that the Iraqis put much more effort into concealment and deception after being caught out in 1981. The important point is that the views of the United Nations in such circumstances have depended not on some detached judgement but on the particular configuration of political forces obtaining at the time. In 1981 Iraq remained close to the Soviet Union, but Western countries, including the United States, were making some effort to wean the country away from its dependence on Moscow, and were also sympathetic to its struggle against Iran. France had actually sold Iraq the reactor in the mid-1970s.

The relevance of this political configuration had been evident the previous year. On the night of 21–22 September 1980 Iraq invaded Iran. This had a pre-emptive justification, in that the new regime in Iran, led by the Ayatollah Khomeini, posed an ideological challenge and was seeking to stir anti-government feelings among Iraq's majority Shia population. Iraqi President Saddam Hussein acted opportunistically, in an effort to take advantage of the tumult within Iran following the overthrow of the Shah. The seven non-aligned members of the Security Council refused to agree to a meeting, having been persuaded by a 'senior Iraqi official, sent from Baghdad for the purpose, that nothing should be done to inhibit what Iraq believed would be a *blitzkrieg* of a few days' duration'. The refusal to blame Iraq for starting the war or even to determine that there had been a technical 'breach of the peace' had important consequences in terms of the international response. If such a determination had been made, then there would have been a requirement to consider mandatory sanctions. The British Ambassador to the United Nations at the time has described the performance of the Security Council in response to the Iraqi invasion of Iran as 'contemptible'. It provided:

> an important gloss on the definition of aggression . . . namely that the international reaction to an armed attack by one state on another is conditioned not so much by the gravity of the act itself but by the international standing and alliances of the victim, and of the aggressor, respectively.[3]

It took more than a decade, until December 1991, when Iraq's international standing had slumped, for the Secretary-General of the United Nations to issue a report which concluded that the Iraqi attack of September 1980 could not be 'justified under the Charter of the United Nations, any recognized rules or any principles of international morality'.[4] Determinations of what is internationally legal and illegal can follow some known principles, but in practice they are also going to be affected by the great power relations of the moment.

When it comes to justifying a pre-emptive doctrine, the USA has referred to legal principles, while reserving the right to deal directly if necessary with all challenges to national security. This includes international terrorism. In 1986, for example, Secretary of State George Schultz observed:

> It is absurd to argue that international law prohibits us from capturing terrorists in international waters or airspace; from attacking them on the soil of other nations, even for the purpose of rescuing hostages; or from using force against states that support, train, and harbour terrorists or guerrillas.[5]

Later that year, as if to make the point, a number of targets in Libya were bombed following an attack on a Berlin nightclub frequented by US servicemen.

The possibility of using military power to nip developing unconventional threats in the bud was explored during the elder Bush's Administration, after the 1991 Persian Gulf War, by Paul Wolfowitz, who was a key figure in the Pentagon (and became Deputy Secretary of Defense under Bush junior) when Richard Cheney was Secretary of Defense (who became Bush junior's Vice-President). Defense Planning Guidance was drafted asserting that the USA would be right to use pre-emptive strikes to stop dangerous states developing weapons of mass destruction, and also to prevent the emergence of any rival superpower in the post-cold war era, presumably China. At the time, this language was thought to be too provocative and it was removed after the draft had been leaked, but the thoughts were still circulating.

In the early 1990s it became apparent that North Korea was attempting to develop nuclear weapons. The Americans made it clear that they were considering some form of attack to remove this option. Eventually, in 1994, a compromise, known as the Agreed Framework, was reached whereby North Korea would abandon this attempt in return for support on civilian nuclear power. In practice this proved difficult to implement. In May 1996, Clinton's Secretary of Defense William J. Perry indicated that it might be necessary to attack another state to interfere with programmes to develop weapons of mass destruction. Again, Libya was the case in mind. Perry declared that a new chemical weapons facility in the desert of Libya 'will not be allowed to begin production', implying that the United States would use military force to secure this promise.[6] The problem in this case was that the relevant facility was located underground and would be hard to attack successfully, and might risk release of deadly materials if it were. Good intelligence would be essential at every level both to justify an attack and then to execute it effectively and safely.

In the 2002 NSS document it was acknowledged that: 'international law recognized that nations need not suffer an attack before they can lawfully take action to defend themselves against forces that present an imminent danger of attack'. But this had been conditional on the existence of an imminent threat – most often a visible mobilization of armies, navies and air forces preparing to attack. Taking this point head on it was asserted that:

> We must adapt the concept of imminent threat to the capabilities and objectives of today's adversaries. Rogue states and terrorists do not seek to attack us using conventional means . . . Instead, they rely on acts of terror and, potentially, the use of weapons of mass destruction – weapons that can easily be concealed, delivered covertly and used without warning.

Furthermore,

> the greater the threat, the greater is the risk of inaction – and the more compelling the case for taking anticipatory action to defend ourselves, even if the uncertainty remains as to the time and place of the enemy's attack. To forestall or prevent such hostile acts by our adversaries, the United States will, if necessary, act preemptively.[7]

Care was taken to provide reassurance that force would not be used 'in all cases to preempt emerging threats'. Nor should others 'use preemption as a pretext for aggression'. The basic point was that the US could not 'remain idle while dangers gather'.[8] The key shift here was the argument that the test should not be one of immediacy, waiting until absolutely the last moment even if this turns out to be too late, but of necessity, acting at the point where an attack can still be forestalled.

It is important to note that the USA was not alone in asserting the possibility of pre-emption. The Australian Prime Minister John Howard spoke about the need to act pre-emptively against terrorists; the head of Japan's Self-defence Agency observed: 'Once North Korea declares it will demolish Tokyo and begins preparing for a missile launch, we will consider it the start of a military attack against Japan.' Even the French agreed that 'the possibility of preemptive action might be considered, from the time that an explicit and

confirmed threatening situation is identified'.[9] Nor were the
Americans taking an extreme stance. In a speech shortly after
the document's release, National Security Advisor Dr
Condoleezza Rice, one of its main architects, developed the
theme of tyrants and terrorists as 'different faces of the same
evil', able, when working together, to magnify the danger
they posed. She went out of her way to deny that there had
been a dramatic policy shift. The new strategy did 'not over-
turn five decades of doctrine and jettison either containment
or deterrence'. The issue was only those threats that were
'so potentially catastrophic – and can arrive with so little
warning, by means that are untraceable – that they cannot
be contained'. For these cases pre-emption was 'not a new
concept. There has never been a moral or legal requirement
that a country wait to be attacked before it can address existential threats.' Even so, Dr Rice agreed that:

> this approach must be treated with great caution. The
> number of cases in which it might be justified will always be
> small. It does not give a green light – to the United States or
> any other nation – to act first without exhausting other
> means, including diplomacy. Preemptive action does not
> come at the beginning of a long chain of effort. The threat
> must be very grave. And the risks of waiting must far out-
> weigh the risks of action.[10]

Regardless, the doctrine was taken further in December 2002
when the administration announced a readiness to use even
nuclear weapons as one form of pre-emption before an
enemy had the chance to unleash weapons of mass destruction. It stated that the United States will 'respond with
overwhelming force', including 'all options', to the use of biological, chemical, radiological or nuclear weapons on the
nation, its troops or its allies. The new strategy did not repu-
diate 'traditional measures' of diplomacy, including multinational arms control agreements and export controls. The
presumption behind the approach was that the established
ways of dealing with the problem of nuclear non-
proliferation had failed and it was therefore necessary to

follow a path of 'active interdiction', which could mean anything from interfering with supplies of deadly materials to
eliminating embryonic arsenals.

Pre-emption in Practice

The NSS document was published at a time when the international focus was on Iraq. The need to deal with radical
powers threatening to gain artificial strength through
weapons of mass destruction had been a high priority for
successive US administrations. Yet the nature of the threat
meant that the framework and vocabulary of the past seemed
inappropriate. While under President Clinton counter-
proliferation policy was at times suggestive of pre-emption,
the public stress was still on deterring rather than eliminating the rogues, so that, for example, policy towards Iraq and
Iran was described as 'dual containment'.

The issue of pre-emption developed in parallel with the
crisis over Iraq's continued defiance of UN resolutions calling
for the elimination of its weapons of mass destruction. The
management of this crisis has therefore been critical to the
development of the pre-emption doctrine. Every other type
of strategy had been tried before with Iraq. The initial strategy of appeasement in the 1980s was undermined by the
cumulative evidence of Saddam Hussein's drive for weapons
of mass destruction, and embarrassing disclosures about the
culpability of Western countries in abetting it. This led to the
rapid deterioration in relations with Iraq during the first
months of 1990 and encouraged Western leaders in their
efforts to deal decisively with Saddam Hussein, even before
Kuwait was occupied in August of that year. Saddam had
shown himself ready to use chemical weapons, against both
the Iranians and the Kurds, and had also mounted missile
attacks against Iranian cities. It was always likely that mass
terror would be part of Iraqi strategy.

Mass terror was not deployed in Iraq's defence during the
1991 Gulf War. Threats were made beforehand to the

regime, warning of dire consequences should such weapons be used, which could be inferred to include nuclear weapons but was most obviously bound up with the overthrow of the regime. Threats were also made to field commanders that they would be considered personally responsible for the con-sequences of chemical use. As chemical weapons were not used by Iraq then, deterrence might have worked, although this might also have been a result of general disorientation and confusion rather than fear of retaliation. Where terror could be used, with Scud missiles and environmental pollu-tion, an attempt was made, albeit to negligible effect. After this came the period of more stringent containment and deterrence, during which it was supposed that as Iraq was much weakened as a result of the war and weighed down with sanctions and UN inspectors, it would cause little trouble. It never appeared at all content with the restrictions under which it was placed, and regularly tested Western resolve to sustain them. As that resolve began to weaken during the 1990s, with Russia and France reluctant to con-tinue with sanctions and inspections, the prospects began to look promising for Saddam Hussein. Even the incoming Bush Administration seemed none too sure about upping the ante. During the 2000 election campaign, George W. Bush's advis-ers showed no inclination to follow this route. Condoleezza Rice, already tipped to be National Security Advisor, took a relatively relaxed line in a *Foreign Affairs* article. She argued that rogue states could be deterred:

> These regimes are living on borrowed time, so there need be no sense of panic about them. Rather, the first line of defense should be a clear and classical statement of deterrence – if they do acquire WMD [weapons of mass destruction], their weapons will be unusable because any attempt to use them will bring national obliteration.[11]

Key administration officials were reluctant to use the 'rogue' language. Prior to the term coming back into the presiden-tial lexicon, Colin Powell had expressed concern about the lack of differentiation implied by 'rogues', and had tried to indicate the key feature of those of concern by referring to their lack of regard for 'international standards of behavior' – that is, norms. He also referred at one point to 'sick' nations, a term that could refer to those beyond deterrence but also in some respects curable. Donald Rumsfeld, when being confirmed as Secretary of Defense, had specifically stated that he did not like the term because it suggested that the regime in question was like 'a rogue elephant, careering off a wall blindly'. He emphasized the rationality of leaders such as Saddam and the late Assad of Syria. He had met them and found them to be 'intelligent, they're survivors, they're tough. . . . They don't think like we do, and goodness knows they don't behave like we do with respect to their neighbors or their own people. But they're not erratic.'[12]

The readiness to believe in the delinquent and the erratic, and to adopt 'rogue state' language, followed 9/11. An influential lobby had been arguing the case for removing Saddam's regime but had made little headway until that day, after which the case gained momentum. In February 2003 President Bush acknowledged the shift, in response to an accusation that he had always wanted to invade Iraq. Prior to 11 September, he observed, 'we were discussing smart sanctions. . . . After September 11, the doctrine of containment just doesn't hold any water. . . . My vision shifted dramatically after September 11, because I now realize the stakes, I realize the world has changed.'[13] Worst-case thinking acquired a new credibility. Terrible things could really happen and suggestions that they might were not necessarily the figments of some fevered strategic imagination.

In President Bush's January 2002 State of the Union address he introduced the notion of an 'axis of evil', including North Korea, Iran and Iraq, as threatening the world with weapons of mass destruction and potentially linked to terrorism. The link became tighter in Bush's West Point speech and the NSS document. The putative enemy appeared as something of a composite, combining the worst features of Saddam Hussein and Osama bin Laden. Saddam had a state,

no hint of any personal interest in martyrdom and a calculating nature, in addition to extreme ruthlessness and an
undoubted fascination with all types of destructive instrument. Even so, at least one proponent of armed action to
remove this threat considered that there was something that
put Saddam beyond deterrence. Kenneth Pollack wrote:

> Saddam has a number of pathologies that make deterring him
> unusually difficult. He is an inveterate gambler and risk-taker
> who regularly twists his calculation of the odds to suit his
> preferred course of action. . . . [He] is fundamentally aggres-
> sive and risk-acceptant. Leaving him free to acquire nuclear
> weapons and then hoping that in spite of his track record he
> can be deterred this time around is not the kind of social
> science experiment the United States government should be
> willing to run.[14]

This was a controversial view. A distinction might be made
between an opponent who takes high risks and one who does
not take risks into account. So long as some sort of risk calculus is being taken, then it can in principle be influenced,
especially when Saddam's risk-taking in the past had been so
disastrous. Providing a threat of greater clarity through
stepped-up rhetoric and military preparations could be taken
as one means of reinforcing deterrence. The question of
deterrability is not new. In the 1960s, for example, Communist China was never presented as a paragon of cautious
stability. During the days of the Cultural Revolution, Mao
Zedong was alleged to be extraordinarily zealous and ready
to take the most catastrophic risks, yet the United States did
not abandon the notion of containment for that reason. It
just recognized that in this case more care had to go into
making the policy work. If adversaries are not dangerous, the
issue of deterrence does not arise in the first place. Some
might be beyond deterrence but that does not mean they are
invariably so. The three 'axes of evil' – North Korea, Iran and
Iraq – had been in dispute with the USA for more than fifty,
twenty and ten years respectively, and, after their initial

challenges to US power, had seemed unwilling to attempt another act of conventional aggression. The reason why deterrence was so difficult in this case was not so much the imminence of the Iraqi threat or the irrationality of the regime, but the American view that the 'Saddam problem' could only truly be solved through the toppling of the regime. This of course made it difficult to coerce the regime, as it was unlikely to agree to demands for its own abolition. Regime change implied control and not coercion.

In addition to the query about whether Iraq could be deterred, there were also the familiar questions about whether precipitate action might make the situation far worse. Many argued that such a policy risked causing more damage than it prevented (the impact on the Middle East, the possibility that before the operation to remove the regime succeeded some of the deadly weapons might be used, the prospect of street fighting in Baghdad, the uncertainty over the sort of regime that could replace that of Saddam Hussein), and others argued that the possibility of containing Iraq was being discounted too easily. At issue also was the question of the precedent. Sir Michael Quinlan, the leading British theorist of deterrence during his period in the Ministry of Defence, argued, in relation to Iraq, that there was no doubt about the malignancy of Saddam's regime or his non-compliance with UN resolutions. Nor would he say that 'pre-emption is never warranted' – only that 'the hurdle must be set very high: the evil needs to be cogently probable as well as severe'. He argued that there was no evidence that the international containment that had held for more than a decade was breaking down. This regime was 'not a shadowy terrorist organization'. Rather, it had 'much to lose – and deterrence can be brought to bear'.[15]

This was the initial response of *New York Times* columnist Thomas Friedman to the 'axis of evil' speech in an article entitled 'Deterrence at Last'. He took issue with European critics of Bush's speech. Yes, Friedman agreed, these countries don't really constitute an axis, and it was best not to drive them together, and the USA should certainly not pretend that it can fight everywhere alone. Still, he argued, the critics were missing the larger point. The terrorist attacks on the United States on 11 September 2001 'happened because America had lost its deterrent capability'. It had been lost because the USA had failed to respond to previous terrorist attacks and had encouraged its enemies to take 'us less and less seriously'. They were emboldened because they thought the USA was 'soft'. Bush was now telling those who might be tempted to harm the USA in the future: 'We don't know exactly what you're cooking in your bathtubs. We don't know exactly what we're going to do about it, but if you think we are going to sit back and take another dose from you, you're wrong.'[16]

By September 2002 Friedman was less sure, because the President was now moving beyond deterrence. Having taken soundings among the American population, Friedman concluded that they considered Saddam to be 'deterrable', but they remained anxious about the 'undeterrables – the terrorists who hate us more than they love their own lives'. Saddam, by contrast, was 'homicidal, not suicidal'. His life had been spent perfecting the art of survival: 'he loves life more than he hates us'.[17] Support for the potential effectiveness of deterrence could be found in Iraq's failure to use chemical weapons during the 1991 war, after clear warnings had been issued that this would lead the Americans to expand their war aims to include the toppling of the regime. If Saddam was now being closely watched for any false move would he really try to hand over weapons to al-Qaeda? Until there was evidence that he had begun to take such steps, any argument to act on the hypothesis that he just might do so would be preventive rather than pre-emptive.

Furthermore, it was unclear whether Iraq was being chosen because it was the most serious threat or because it was the most accessible. It had already firmly acquired the status of an international outlaw, was subject to numerous UN resolutions and sanctions, and was not in the best military shape, whatever its hidden or future potential might be. If the most dangerous of the 'axis' countries was to be chosen, it would probably be North Korea. While Iraq was denying pursuing illicit WMD projects, North Korea was cheerfully admitting to such projects, and indeed was believed to have a couple of rudimentary nuclear weapons. In 1994, then-Secretary of Defense William Perry stated publicly that the United States would not allow North Korea to develop a nuclear arsenal (although the administration issued no explicit threat to use force). This threat may have had an effect, in that Pyongyang agreed to cap its nuclear programme, although it was subsequently discovered that this was less than the whole truth. It still remained in violation of a particular promise and its commitments under the non-proliferation treaty. The North Korean case met, even more than the Iraqi, the criteria raised in the West Point speech – that is, the failure of containment when 'unbalanced dictators with weapons of mass destruction can deliver those weapons on missiles or secretly provide them to terrorist allies'.[18] Yet containment appeared as the best option with North Korea, given its ability to strike South Korea (with conventional artillery as much as nuclear weapons) as well as Japan, even if the offending reprocessing facility at Yongbon could be destroyed without releasing radioactive materials.

This confirms the extent to which the new doctrine was preventive rather than truly pre-emptive, because it relied on the opponent being so weak that it would be unable to retaliate immediately, with the threat in the future rather than the present. Another difficulty emerged with the bold pre-emptive doctrine, when an opportunity came to implement that aspect of it which targeted the transfer of deadly technologies, a trade in which North Korea was known to indulge. In December 2002, Spanish special forces, with US intelligence support, stopped a North Korean ship in the Arabian sea bound for Yemen with 15 North Korean Scud missiles, 15 conventional warheads, 23 containers of nitric acid fuel and 85 barrels of unidentified chemicals hidden under a cargo of cement. Unfortunately for the Spanish and the Americans, neither the cargo nor the trade was actually illegal, and eventually the ship had to be allowed to go on its way.

All this confirmed that it was difficult to operationalize pre-emption as a strategic concept. In a 1995 article Dan Reiter noted that, other than the special case of the First World War, pre-emptive action is unusual, with Israel's 1967 war and the Chinese intervention in Korea as rare examples.[19] Pre-emption, he noted, was more likely to be motivated by fear than greed. Furthermore, he confirmed that this was another taboo, that constraints on pre-emption were 'driven by ideas rather than by material structure'. The political costs of pre-emption could be traced to 'the idea that pre-emption is undesirable', and this could be 'enforced by third parties through threats of withholding aid'. Alternatively, 'certain ways of thinking about war, and in particular the spiral model of action and counter-reaction, could create a self-denying prophecy that would inhibit leaders when contemplating pre-emption'.[20] This leads to a practical point for, as Bunn notes, when there really is a threat of imminent use by the enemy, 'the easier pre-emption is to justify politically, but the harder it will be to be operationally decisive'.[21]

The importance of the normative element came out in a careful critique of the Bush doctrine for the Brookings Institution. O'Hanlon, Rice and Steinberg noted that the United States 'did not need a formal doctrine of preemption' to drive home the need to take a strong stand against terrorism and extremism. Furthermore, by developing pre-emption as a right, it was being made available to others. It could become a 'hunting license' for others.[22] The same doctrine appeared already to be in use as Russia claimed its rights against Georgia, while China threatened to act to stop the Taiwanese from ruling out eventual reunification. India appeared as one of the most enthusiastic supporters of the new approach, conscious of how it might be useful if Pakistan had to be disciplined for failing to stop terrorists opposing the Indian position in Kashmir. Thus the revision of international norms in one context could create opportunities for other states elsewhere.

At the same time, other states with a more cautious approach to international affairs might take fright if it

appeared that the Americans – and other large states – were
gaining extra latitude to throw their weight around with only
scant regard for international law. If it was the case, as Condoleezza Rice had suggested, that an objective of American
policy was to 'dissuade any potential adversary from pursuing a military build-up in the hope of surpassing, or equalling,
the power of the United States and our allies' – that is, sustain
its military hegemony – then that would be a recipe for con-
tinual preventive wars, potentially leading to ever more desperate measures by those with reason to fear such wars.[23]
This notion of dissuasion, which Rice did not define, is similar
to but not quite the same as deterrence. Dissuasion would
normally be taken to incorporate all forms of persuasion,
including reassurances and inducements, that would lead a
target not to follow a particular course of action. Nonetheless, the new doctrine reinforced the developing image of the
United States as a country that insisted that it should be
exempted from the disciplines of international norms even
while others should accede to them.

In addition, by leading the adversary to expect trouble, it
might encourage them to put their efforts into concealment
and defensive preparations as well as into disarmament. Nor
was it even the case that the Iraq War of 2003 was properly
described as pre-emptive. The cause of war was not an *imminent* attack by Iraq on the USA or its allies; if it had been,
the pathetic state of Iraqi military preparations revealed by
the war would have cast doubt on the justification. The claim
was that Iraq was getting into a position where it could be
dangerous, but the embarrassing failure to find substantial
evidence of chemical or biological weapons provided retro-
spective question-marks against this rationale, and indeed
will be used as grounds for caution should a similar rationale be used as grounds for attack against another state. The
legal case depended on UN resolutions going back to 1990
and their systematic defiance. The political case, once the war
was over, depended increasingly on the dreadful nature of
Saddam Hussein's regime and the evident relief of ordinary
Iraqis at its overthrow. This may have been a justification for

war, but it followed a quite different track to pre-emption. It meant that the stress on the imperatives of national security that had been so prominent prior to the war gave way to more explicitly normative rationales based on human rights and the removal of an obnoxious regime.

All this suggests that there was less to the new doctrine than met the eye. At one level, pre-emption was just one option among many and certainly did not exclude deterrence. The NSS document affirmed the need to strengthen 'America's homeland security to protect against and deter attack'. In more familiar terms, the US military was still required to 'deter threats against US interests, allies, and friends; and decisively defeat any adversary if deterrence fails'.[24] An official, speaking anonymously, agreed that deterrence and pre-emption were not necessarily incompatible, in that knowing that such direct action was possible, it would be wise not to provide the USA with a pretext. 'There is also a deterrent element for the bad guys.'[25] Talking about pre-emption in advance was a means of issuing a warning not to act in a certain way, although strictly speaking if a threat were truly imminent so that any delay would mean disaster, then there would be no time to talk and wait to assess its effects.

If the USA were to indicate that it was prepared to use military action when it judged it appropriate, then those that might be on the receiving end would be advised to moderate their behaviour to deny Washington pretexts. Yet if force were to be used without the pretext of imminent aggressive action, or even evidence that it is contemplated, then it is hard to say that deterrence and containment are proven to be inadequate. If facilities are attacked and regimes are overthrown before these dangers have a chance to emerge, that will be described as pre-emption, because that is the language currently in vogue. But it would be incorrect. The relevant concept is prevention.

Furthermore, the descriptions of pre-emption in the NSS document suggest that the concept can be considered more broadly than just military strikes, in the softer fields of sharper intelligence work, diplomatic attention, and judicious applications of economic assistance, technical advice and military/police support. In terms of a prudent and effective approach to the war on terror, this makes sense, providing good guidance for dealing with the security problems within and arising from weak states. But again in this context, prevention is more the issue than pre-emption – acting early rather than late, while a problem gestates but before it erupts, using all available means. There will of course be instances when a terrorist attack is imminent and where a quick, pre-emptive strike would be appropriate, but deterrence is not necessarily impossible in such circumstances (as in the claims that public warnings about imminent attacks have served to warn off those planning them) and the action to be taken is more likely to involve the police than the armed forces. In circumstances where pre-emptive strikes of a traditional sort might be justified, the old tests will still apply: making sure that action heads off danger rather than aggravates or instigates it.

This might be described as preventative rather than pre-emptive, but not in the sense of preventive war. 'Conflict prevention' has normally referred to diplomatic more than military action, using all available instruments to calm an area of conflict, after getting early warning of developing tension, and encouraging the search for a long-term resolution. At some point this could be pre-emptive, for example with the ultimatum against Serbia in a belated effort to prevent the persecution of the local Albanians. By and large, however, the great powers got involved when fighting was already under way, humanitarian catastrophes loomed or neighbouring countries risked getting dragged in. Few of these conflicts even started with a classic military offensive, but emerged out of intercommunal violence.

There are good reasons why the United States and its allies would prefer not to wait for problems to reach a critical stage before they are tackled. So long as you are sure of your diagnosis, 'prevention is better than cure' is as good a motto for foreign policy as it is for medicine. Unfortunately, diagnosis is no small test when considering political processes, which could develop in a number of ways, rather than incipient disease. At best, in contemporary conditions, diagnosis requires close attention to what is going on in the disadvantaged and disaffected parts of the international system, and consideration of the full range of policy instruments. The enthusiasm for pre-emption reflects a yearning for a world in which problems can be eliminated by some bold, timely and decisive strokes. The cases where this can happen are likely to be few and far between. An updated notion of prevention, by contrast, might encourage recognition that the world we have is one in which the best results are likely to come from a readiness to engage with difficult problems over an extended period.

The new, dynamic and unsettled international environment has exposed the limits of a conceptual framework derived from a period when international politics was dominated by great power rivalries and international law gave overriding respect to the rights of states, no matter how brutal their internal policies. It has also challenged assumptions about the use of force. The prominence given to preemptive possibilities by the Bush Administration seems less significant when the surrounding explanations and qualifications are examined, as they reveal an unexceptional set of propositions, remote from the belligerent tone of the more simplistic presentations. Even so, they represent a challenge to common assumptions. Other than territorial expansion, where the proscriptive norm appears firmly established, there is no obvious relationship between actual state practice and the framework embedded in the UN Charter. Michael Glennon, for example, has challenged the notion that any 'customary norm of state practice constrains the use of force'. He notes:

> Between 1945 and 1999, two-thirds of the members of the United Nations – 126 states out of 189 – fought 291 interstate conflicts in which over 22 million people were killed. This series of conflicts was capped by the Kosovo campaign in which nineteen NATO democracies representing 780 million people flagrantly violated the Charter.

From this, he concludes that two parallel systems now exist in the international system: one de jure, consisting 'of illusory rules that would govern that use of force among states in a platonic world of forms'; and the other de facto, consisting 'of actual state practice in the real world, a world in which states weigh costs against benefits in regular disregard of the rules solemnly proclaimed in the all-but-ignored de jure system'. On this basis, he argues that the Charter can no longer serve as a guide for responsible policy-makers.[26] After almost sixty years of change, passing through the end of colonialism and the whole cold war and taking in the rise of international terrorism, it would be strange if the Charter formulations did not appear dated. The underlying presumption that international order requires clear restraints on the use of force, and that its most legitimate use, even in anticipation, is in response to hostile acts by others remains valid. The question becomes one of the form in which those hostile acts are defined and whether there can be a developing consensus, at least among the major powers, about how best to respond. The presentation of the case for pre-emption in 2002 and the war against Iraq the following year encouraged the view that these matters would be decided unilaterally by the United States, but the Bush Administration never quite turned its back on multilateralism, and the aftermath of the war in Iraq demonstrated the advantages of working as part of a wider coalition. This in turn requires it to make its case in more universal terms. As Charles Kegley and Gregory Raymond point out, as the reigning hegemony the United States cannot follow one code of conduct and expect others to follow another. If it wants to encourage a restrictive normative framework when it comes to the use of force, then it cannot claim a permissive one for itself.[27]

This issue of the use of force can be taken further by considering the other traditional concept in which there has been revived interest since the end of the cold war.

Compellence

Deterrence is concerned with discouraging others from acting in ways that advantage them but harm you. Strategies geared to coercing others to act in ways they might consider harmful but advantage you have been described as compellence or coercive diplomacy. The first term derives from the 'second-wave' theorist, Tom Schelling, and the second from a team led by the 'third-wave' Alexander George and William Simon. Both originated during the cold war. Schelling's 1966 book *Arms and Influence* reflected his interest in the persuasive power of armed force.[1] George and Simon, writing after armed force had proved to be less than persuasive in Vietnam, entitled their 1970 book *The Limits of Coercive Diplomacy*.[2] In a volume I edited in 1997, I acknowledged the enormous value of both books but suggested, with my contributors, that they were too focused on the strategic choices of states in general and of the United States in particular. The line between politics within states and between states was blurring, so theory needed to consider the employment of strategic threats by any politically conscious collectivity for a great variety of potential purposes, and not just by states, let alone just by great powers.[3]

According to Schelling, whereas deterrence was about 'inducing inaction', obliging the opponent, against his will, not to do something that he wanted to do, compellence required 'making someone perform', that is doing – or undoing – something against his will. With deterrence, B must be persuaded not to do something. Having explained what this is, and the consequences of non-compliance, A can only wait to see what, if anything, B gets up to. With compellence, in contrast, A sets in motion a train of events that will only be concluded when B responds to A's satisfaction. The most important difference between them is that deterrence upholds a status quo whereas compellence is more radical, requiring movement to 'a destination, and the destination can be unclear in intent as well as in momentum and braking power'.[4] It therefore lacks the limits of deterrence and is much more difficult to achieve and then manage. In addition, while with deterrence compliance is literally a non-event and therefore does not necessarily require any special rationalization by the deterred, with compellence, compliance will be blatant, and therefore carry with it the added reputational significance of humiliation.

Alexander George has a similar idea to Schelling:

> The general intent of coercive diplomacy is to back a demand on an adversary with a threat of punishment for noncompliance that will be credible and potent enough to persuade him that it is in his interest to comply with the demand.[5]

Whether or not compliance can be achieved will depend on the significance of A's demand, B's determination and on an assessment as to the credibility and potency of the threatened punishment. A can improve the chances of success by the care with which demands are framed, creating a sense of urgency, the choice of punishment, the addition of positive inducements, a readiness to make changes as a crisis unfolds, adding or increasing the sense of urgency, changing the form and scale of military deployments, adding or subtracting from the punishments and introducing forms of inducement and reassurance. As mentioned earlier, when considering what makes for success, George puts a great stress on 'asymmetry of motivation', and in particular what is believed by B about A's motivation. He concludes, with Simon, that coercive diplomacy can constitute 'a high-confidence strategy in few crises', but is often difficult to 'employ successfully against a recalcitrant or unpredictable opponent'.[6]

The distinction between deterrence and compellence is not necessarily sharp, and George appears to see coercive diplomacy on a spectrum with deterrence. The main difference is the time pressure. If the objective is for nothing to happen, then the time horizon can be indefinite; if the objective is that something should happen, then timing is crucial, which is why compellence tends to be associated with ultimatums. The two might merge when B starts doing something A has urged it not to do in the first place and the situation has to be retrieved. Another example might be a conflict in which both sides can hurt each other but neither can force matters to a decisive conclusion. It appears compellent to one side, deterrent to the other. Once an engagement has begun, the difference between the two, like the difference between defence and offence, may disappear. Indeed, this is the basis of the whole problem of the credibility of deterrence. Consider the Cuban Missile Crisis of October 1962. The United States was warning the Soviet Union at the same time to stop constructing missile sites in Cuba (compellence) and not to pass ships carrying more missiles through the American blockade (deterrence). When it was deciding what to do, the Soviet Government warned Washington in turn that if its threats were implemented then terrible consequences would result. This was therefore a process of coercion and counter-coercion with deterrence and compellence under way on both sides at the same time.

It could be added that if the USA had been moved to strike at the missile bases in Cuba, this would have been an act of pre-emption. When the strong is deterring the weak, without any possibility of counter-coercion, then credibility may not be a large problem. But once this capacity exists, which was the case throughout the cold war, then every deterrence threat carries with it a secondary issue of compellence. Once the threat fails, the tables are turned, and the roles of deter-rer and compeller are reversed. So while the conceptual issues are being discussed in terms of B being the recipient of A's conditional threats, it is important to note that it is quite possible for both to be seeking to implement coercive strategies at the same time.

Strategic Coercion

In *Strategic Coercion* (a concept which explicitly includes deterrence) the case studies indicated the extent to which a one-way power relationship is unusual. In most strategic rela-tionships B has resources available with which to attempt to counter-coerce A. Strategic coercion normally involves a two-way traffic in threats. In addition, the relationships of which they are a part will probably include areas of cooper-ation as well as conflict. They will also be part of a sequence. This may involve the development of the core strategic relationship between the main protagonists, but it can also involve other types of connection, for example where A puts pressure on B to bring client C to heel. An example of this would be the pressure NATO countries put on Yugoslavia's Slobodan Milosevic to persuade the Bosnian Serbs to make the concessions necessary to get a political settlement, or the pressure Israel has put on the Palestinian Authority to deal with the radical militants. Another aspect of inter-connectedness comes when B, in order to resist A's coercion (or possibly to initiate coercion of its own), draws in D, another, stronger actor. The reason that Milosevic was under pressure with Bosnia was because the Bosnian Government had worked hard to convince Western governments that they were the victims of unacceptable behaviour. The more actors involved in a coercive activity, the more complex it may become, as bargaining within the group complicates bargaining between the coercer and the coerced. During the course of a conflict, A will receive feedback in the form of B's response to its threats and may have to modify its views accordingly. Eventually, it may realize that it has been guilty of a monumental misapprehension. Alternatively, it may have got the measure of B from the start.

A coercive process is potentially extremely dynamic. Once force has been invoked, a new issue is introduced to a strategic relationship, for even if this does not move beyond threats, the memory of a readiness to cause hurt will still remain. Once force has been used, attitudes are apt to harden and compromise becomes harder. Alternatively, the coercive act may demonstrate that the relationship is so unequal that B will recognize that there is little choice but to seek an accommodation with A. The very fact that A understands that B cannot be controlled, and will retain an element of choice, is in itself a recognition of B's likely durability as an independent entity and the possible need to establish a different kind of relationship once the immediate crisis has passed. Should an accommodation be reached, A will be looking for signs that B is truly committed to its implementation, and has not just made an expedient compromise to ease the immediate pressure. Iraq accepted an unfavourable compromise with Iran over the Shatt-al-Arab waterway in 1975. As soon as Iraq detected weakness in Iran, in 1980, the attempt was made to get the agreement reversed.

The situations being described, therefore, are those in which strategic actors are trying to sort out their differences, aware of the potential impact of their conduct on other actors and their long-term reputations, even if it is difficult to be precise. As the conflict develops, its character will change and adjustments will have to be made. In times such as these, states are obliged to come clean on what is of central importance to them and what is peripheral. These interests may well be reappraised continually in the light of changing circumstances, with the costs and risks of attending to one set of interests constituting an interest in themselves, and new interests will develop beyond those which prompted the crisis in the first place. In 1999 in Kosovo, for example, because it was NATO that issued the threat rather than individual countries, the credibility of the organization as a security provider for Europe was soon in question. Individual states had to consider the implications of walking away from the conflict with Serbia for the integrity of this vital organization.

Thus, formulating an interest is by no means straightforward. Interests are not, as is so often assumed in international relations, straightforward and unchanging, simple price-tags attached to pieces of territory or to friendly states or political principles, that give a value to set against the costs of acting to secure them. Prior to a crisis, A may have been much clearer about interests with the friendly C or the dependent D than with the potentially hostile B. Adopting a coercive strategy requires that A clarifies the meaning and ramifications of alternative options in circumstances of great uncertainty, and possibly low initial salience, if A itself is not directly at risk. This process of sorting out interests is therefore as important as the attempt to work out what, potentially, B is up to, and what it may take to persuade B to change to a comparatively benign course. Even when interests are discerned in new and unique situations, questions of investment and logistics will loom large. If a threat is to be credible, then it must be possible to use armed force in relevant ways. Questions of bases and troop deployments were thus critical to the US discussions with the Saudi Arabians in August 1990, after the Iraqi invasion of Kuwait, which concluded with US troops moving to Saudi Arabia. Whether or not this was necessary to stop an Iraqi invasion of Saudi Arabia, it did serve to reassure the Saudis and prevent them from adopting an appeasement strategy in relation to Iraq, while bringing home to the international community the seriousness of the situation and creating future options for a compellent strategy to remove Iraq from Kuwait. But then later, after the war, the continuing US presence in Saudi Arabia took on a quite different aspect, denounced by Osama bin Laden as a provocation to Islam and the target of terrorists. By the time of the 2003 war, the USA saw the Saudi garrison as more of a liability than an asset, and steps were taken to remove it as soon as Saddam was overthrown.

Thus questions of threat and counter-threat, warnings of force to come and its actual use, and assertions about interests and norms are all context-dependent and change over time. The multifaceted nature of strategic relationships requires accommodating a variety of pressures and considering a range of possible responses. Governments may incline towards certain types of strategic posture, or at least acquire a reputation for being too trigger-happy or too soft, but in the end whether they opt to coerce, control or conciliate will depend on their assessments of the situations in which they find themselves, in all their complexity.

8   THE FUTURE OF DETERRENCE

Deterrence can be a technique, a doctrine and a state of mind. In all cases it is about setting boundaries for actions and establishing the risks associated with the crossing of those boundaries. These are key activities in all societies. In international relations these activities dominate diplomatic activity and military provisions. During the cold war, this effort became focused on the superpower confrontation, dominated by nuclear deterrence, to the point where it sucked in all theory. The study of deterrence became synonymous with the study of the strategic conduct of the cold war. The confrontation defined the concept rather than the concept the confrontation.

Now that the concept is no longer dominant, individual diplomatic or military moves have to be justified in their own terms. There is reluctance to give a high salience to nuclear weapons or to claim that only these weapons stand between the United States and some sort of strategic defeat. For most of the time deterrence is marginal, tangential or speculative. As a strategy, it provides one option among many, possibly appropriate in particular circumstances. Deterrence helps explain why certain strategic moves are assessed to be foreclosed by frustrated states and why others are deemed essential by fearful states. For practitioners facing an immediate challenge, the best advice must be to draw on some careful empirical work on the situation at hand as much as on any work of theory. Even then there is no guarantee of success. Precisely because they depend in the end on the cooperation of opponents, all deterrence-based strategies are subject to doubt.[1] Even if all the successful acts of deterrence were explicit enough to be gathered together for analysis, the enormous variety of situations covered would defeat any attempt to establish a general theory.

It is certainly possible to come up with propositions about when, in particular conditions, certain types of deterrence are more or less likely to work. But the concept requires considerable differentiation, according to the ambition of the task, the numbers of actors involved and the degree of the antagonism. Students of international relations may find this interesting and worthwhile, but practitioners may find it frustrating, as it provides little reliable guidance for policy other than to suggest that close attention is paid to the specifics of a situation rather than a reliance on vague generalizations. We have seen how complicated a theoretical tangle developed around deterrence even during the cold war, a period of unusual clarity and continuity in international affairs. The end of the cold war seemed bound to add to the tangle and provide few opportunities for any unravelling. Morgan concludes his latest book by observing:

> While certain abstract elements of deterrence have something of a universal character, the degree and nature of its challenges and implementation are so uneven and varied, the operational conceptions of deterrence and the specifics of both challenge and response are so elaborate, that it is inevitably lodged in the varying national and political character of conflicts, shaped by the social and cultural detail of the motivations, perceptions, and analyses that drive challenges and responses.

Deterrence is 'not sufficiently consistent to be captured by our theoretical apparatus and empirical studies'.[2]

It is hard to argue with this. There may still be a way forward, indicated by the analysis of the underlying concept, and the debates surrounding apparently related concepts such as compellence and pre-emption. I have argued that acts of deterrence cannot be separated out from the wider context of relations which shape them and give them meaning, or from the stream of history, which draws on past acts and builds on the meaning that new acts acquire. So deterrence serves as a boundary-setting activity, but only one of a number of related activities. When A wishes to establish its claim to a piece of land which is at the same time claimed by B, it does not simply make threats about the consequences should B set foot on this land, but takes steps to make these threats credible. A will also ensure that C, D and E, when they have dealings with A, have little choice but to recognize the claim, so that it acquires an inherent legitimacy that makes it harder for B to assert a contrary claim. As an example, consider Britain's failure to deter the Argentine occupation of the Falklands in 1982. In part this was because of the puny military capability in the South Atlantic, incapable of resisting an Argentine invasion, but it was also because of its inability to convince Latin American opinion, or the UN General Assembly, of the quality of its claim, and the apparent half-heartedness with which it dealt with the economic and social development of the Islands.

Thus, when using deterrence to defend an interest, it is necessary not only to demonstrate how deterrence will work if challenged but also the nature of the interest to be defended. This is why extended deterrence could appear to be so problematic, because the risks that might be run when a sovereign territory is under attack are unlikely to be as great when the territory of an ally is under threat, or that of some new friend with whom the only thing in common is a shared enemy. What we need to think about is not so much how to make deterrence work, but about what sorts of behaviour we now wish to proscribe, and what role deterrence measures can play in this effort.

While I have argued the possibility of deterrence as part of an effort to develop and reinforce a normative framework, it is important to be aware of the limits of what is being suggested. The rhetorical flourishes of the moment may encourage a vision of a democratic and just world, but armed force can only help in a negative sense, by demonstrating abhorrence of those practices that are most inimical to human rights, and hardly at all in a positive sense, by demonstrating the virtues of liberal democracy in practice. If Western values are to take root, much more fundamental and long-term change will be required in individual societies. In addition, it will be difficult to develop a framework when key norms are in contention. To take one example, a 1981 Executive Order states: 'No person employed by or acting on behalf of the United States shall engage in or conspire to engage in assassination.' Part of the case against Saddam Hussein was the alleged attempt to assassinate the first President Bush in 1993. Yet extra-judicial killing often commends itself to governments frustrated in their ability to deal with covert groups, and concerns about terrorism were used to argue for the repeal of this Executive Order. Leaving aside the question of whether such killings can be counter-productive, for example in creating martyrs, the larger point is that sustaining a norm means eschewing options that might have some opportunistic temptation.

The wider objective therefore has to be to encourage the development of an international order in which there are formidable restraints on the use of force, and where the main legitimate role of force is to enforce these restraints. In this regard much has already been achieved. In the post-cold war condition of US/Western military hegemony and relative territorial security, states contemplating action that would be judged hostile by the USA have already had to accept limits on their freedom of manoeuvre. Here the costs of deterrence are tangible but not large. Indeed, the United States can feel that now it can deter not only nuclear war against its territory but also conventional war elsewhere, for example across the Taiwan Straits.[3] In other areas, the ability to exercise this form of deterrence may be restricted by either limited interest in outcomes or the possibilities of counter-deterrence, as a result, for example, of nuclear proliferation. In these cases, however, it may be that more localized systems of mutual deterrence, along traditional cold war lines, might develop.[4] Counter-arguments point to the difficulties of developing elsewhere the particular combination of antagonism and cooperation which led to stability in the East–West nuclear relationship, especially in areas of greater fluidity and tension. In areas such as South Asia and the Middle East, the presence of local nuclear powers may dampen down tendencies towards conflict, though at the same time it renders those that defy the dampening process potentially far more dangerous. The Indo-Pakistani case study remains the most formidable test of the optimistic view that nuclear weapons can encourage caution all round. So far it has worked, although it is hard to be confident about the margin of error.[5]

The issue here is not whether there is reason for Western states to intervene, but the extent to which they will be inhibited by the existence of these capabilities. A credible threat of WMD from rogue states or terrorists might persuade the United States to intervene in some parts of the world, and for this reason it has maintained a full deterrent threat, even including nuclear use, to persuade potential enemies not even to think about such a move. Thus far it has succeeded, although the occasions when this might have been tested have been few. There are of course a number of reasons why this appears a less attractive option than might be assumed. The 'WMD' designation can be seriously misleading. Actual chemical use (even against civilian targets) may turn out to be feeble in its effects, because of the protective measures taken, or the ineffectual dispersion of the agents, or their misdirection. Regardless, the horror associated with the use of such weapons, and long-standing international measures designed to ban their use and prohibit their employment, have led to a degree of stigmatization that would appear to justify a harsh response (which would not have to be retaliation in kind). Nuclear weapons fit unambiguously into the WMD category and may always provide a degree of deterrence for those who have them. They may help North Korea stand up to external pressures, although they will be of little use to the ruling regime as it copes with its own inner decay. Nuclear weapons remain the most awesome disciplinary instrument around, but the unimaginable consequences of their use still acts as a powerful inhibition. The first to break the 'nuclear taboo' will want to be very sure that all other options have been exhausted.

The big fear has been that a 'rogue' state would hand weapons over to terrorist groups. This was indeed the underlying rationale for the 2003 war against Iraq. Looking back at this rationale, and at the failure to establish a link between Saddam Hussein's regime and al-Qaeda, Steve Simon and Daniel Benjamin have demonstrated that in this area deterrence may already have been working remarkably effectively because 'the world's leading state sponsors of terrorism' lost confidence in their ability to 'carry out attacks against the United States undetected':

> After it became clear to Libya that the United States could prove its responsibility for the 1988 attack on Pan Am 103 – and United Nations sanctions were imposed – it got out of the business of supporting attacks on Americans. After American and Kuwaiti intelligence traced a plot to kill former President George H. W. Bush in 1993 to Baghdad, the Iraqi regime also stopped trying to carry out terrorist attacks against America. And when the Clinton administration made clear that it knew Iran was behind the 1996 bombing of Khobar Towers in Saudi Arabia, Tehran ceased plotting terrorist strikes against American interests.

As a result 'this brand of terrorism has been on the wane'.[6]

Most terrorism involves prolonged and wearying campaigns of harassment and hurt, eating away at political authority as it fails to prevent attacks or deal with the perpetrators, until it becomes obliged to seek some political deal. It is a coercive strategy, as is deterrence, and terrorists too can enjoy the benefits of deterrence. This is evident when it is argued that certain, possibly provocative, actions should be avoided lest they trigger renewed attacks. When people watch what they say and do because they do not want to attract the attention of terrorists, that is a form of deterrence at work. Anything that generates caution and apprehension has possible deterrent effects, even when the behaviour to be avoided has to be inferred. Terrorists can achieve this if they can acquire a reputation for irresistibility. The evidence suggests that they are most likely to achieve this when their campaigns are rooted in the aspirations of a distinctive and aggrieved community, as in Northern Ireland or Palestine. With such campaigns, the damage caused by individual attacks is less important than their regularity. When coupled with manifestos and more normal political activity by sympathetic groups over time, some understanding is created of what this cause is about and the possibilities for its satisfaction. This confirms the view that deterrence arises out of processes in which all involved are learning about what matters to others and their patterns of behaviour.

Al-Qaeda developed a more ambitious strategy during the 1990s, aiming for large and dramatic one-off attacks, with a global rather than a local impact, in the hope of obtaining commensurate political effects. It creates a difficulty in developing responses, even of the appeasing sort, when no clear or consistent patterns of behaviour emerge. If they have no purposes other than causing death and destruction, then the failure to produce advantageous political effects may not bother them. With al-Qaeda-type terrorists, this may be as much of a problem as their suicidal nature. There are obvious problems in using threats of punishment against rootless terrorists, and these are compounded by the terrorists' indifference to their own lives. Furthermore, a vigorous response is actually what the terrorists want, in that it will radicalize those who happen to get in the way and become victims of 'collateral damage'. Lastly, there is no obvious room for compromise, and forms of communication may be non-existent, not least because of the disparate and diffuse nature of the adversary, and those that exist may be subject to suspicion and disbelief. On this basis the National Academies Panel concluded that traditional direct deterrence was impossible, but that forms of communication might be sustained with states who do have some contacts with terrorist supporters and may be able to work to moderate the more vicious elements of their ideologies.[7] In effect this is a strategy that requires isolating terrorists as much as rooting them out through force, and achieving this through stigmatizing their ideas amongst communities that might be sympathetic.

This indirect approach is not necessarily incompatible with a direct approach. When al-Qaeda attacked the United States in September 2001 retaliation was sure and swift. Because it was a loose and dispersed terrorist group, the defeat of al-Qaeda could never be definitive, but it is notable that the main effect of its audacious attack was to push US foreign policy in exactly the opposite direction to the one intended, with two Muslim countries (Afghanistan and Iraq) soon successfully invaded and setbacks in the anti-Indian and anti-Zionist struggles proclaimed by Osama bin Laden, al-Qaeda's founder.

Furthermore, 9/11 had in itself alerted authorities around the world to the dangers of such attacks and set in motion a massive counter-terrorism effort, taking in improved intelligence efforts and international collaboration, increased police powers, tougher sentencing and far more care with the security of air transportation or large public events. The impact of the blows struck against the al-Qaeda network was that terrorist activity became more visceral but less strategic, more retributive and less coercive, more the result of local organization and less of central direction. There were no spectacular strikes against large targets in Western countries but, instead, spasmodic but deadly attacks against soft targets in Muslim countries (Indonesia, Saudi Arabia, Turkey). When a strong reaction was expected, at the time of the US/UK invasion of Iraq, nothing much happened until after the event.

The militants may yet achieve another 9/11, but over time, doubts can be inserted into the minds of would-be terrorists that this particular method of promoting their cause was turning out to be less effective than they might have expected. So while it might be true that it is impossible, in an immediate sense, to deter someone bent on suicide through threats of punishment, that person might be deterred if it transpires that suicides rarely succeed in inflicting much damage or in producing the strategic effects that might justify the martyrdom. To be a suicide bomber is not to say that life is worthless, only that it is worth sacrificing for a good cause. As Robert Pape has convincingly argued, suicide terrorism has been adopted because it appears to work in driving Westerners away from places where they are not welcome.[8] If the effect is unlikely to be achieved, then it is not worth the attempt. With terrorists who are less inclined to martyrdom, the strategic conclusions may be even more profound.

So the argument that deterrence does not work with terrorism can be challenged, not because for every terrorist challenge a sure-fire form of deterrence can be devised, but because over time it becomes apparent that this is a threat for which the community has made adequate provision to the point where, even if some attacks succeed, little of political consequence will follow and those responsible can expect that they will be hounded down and punished. In criminological language (and this is an area that crosses from criminology to international affairs) terrorists and those that support them become stigmatized by the wider community as deviants, and are treated accordingly. It will be recalled from the earlier discussion of the criminological literature on general deterrence that establishing norms in this way, through a number of means including appropriate punishments, can help move communities away from what comes to be perceived to be anti-social activity. A sub-culture that sees this activity as the norm rather than as deviant may prove to be resistant, but when this is a matter not so much of alternative lifestyles but rather of struggles for political control and authority, then containment rather than elimination is often sufficient.

We can see this process at work with ethno-nationalism, another form of deviant behaviour according to the prevailing norms of the international community, especially when it leads to the outrages of 'ethnic cleansing' as were seen in Africa and the former Yugoslavia during the 1990s. Clearly there was no semblance of deterrence in these conflicts, as Croats and Bosnian Muslims (and later Serbs) were brutalized and forced from their homes, and a terrible genocide was set in motion in Rwanda. If anything, deterrence worked in another direction, as the British and French governments sought to restrain tough action against the Serbs in Bosnia because of the vulnerability of their own lightly armed forces, sent in to distribute humanitarian aid, to retaliation. The USA gave up on Somalia in 1993 after eighteen Rangers were conspicuously killed (albeit along with some thousand Somalis) on the streets of Mogadishu, and then stayed clear of Rwanda in 1994. There, extremist Hutus took their cues from Somalia when they murdered ten Belgian troops with the small UN force as a (successful) act of deterrence, before embarking on a genocidal campaign. Even after interventions in Bosnia had brought the parties to a peace settlement, Serb leader Slobodan Milosevic did not accept NATO's warnings made on behalf of the Kosovar Albanians. This became an example of successful coercion, but hardly deterrence. In Iraq, even after fighting a war against the regime in 1991, little was done to protect the Kurds when they faced an onslaught from Iraqi troops following a failed insurrection in March/April 1991, although eventually safe havens were established which were sustained until the regime itself was overthrown in 2003.

There was therefore a process of establishing a norm opposed to ethnic cleansing, including the right of members of the international community to intervene when this norm was being violated. The most egregious violators did not stay in power and some but not all of the worst excesses were mitigated. Some of those responsible have had to face international courts investigating war crimes. Whether it is sufficiently well established that would-be violators are now deterred is unclear. The elements of counter-coercion will remain strong, in that meddling in these conflicts can be dangerous and painful for those inclined to intervene. Moreover, their origins do not necessarily lie in unscrupulous political leaders, who will have to calculate the costs and benefits of stirring up ethnic conflict, but in traditional enmities that may flare up into inter-communal violence through the activities of local hot-heads. A further problem is that an awareness of the value of 'victim status' as a means of gaining international support may lead political leaders of a vulnerable group to aggravate a crisis precisely to draw in outsiders on their behalf. Then there remains the contrary norm of non-interference in internal affairs, which still has many supporters, not least among those who fear that they might be vulnerable should this norm come to be regularly disregarded. At what point does authoritarianism in government turn into systematic repression and begin to demand an international response, as for example with Zimbabwe under Robert Mugabe? It might be the case that a norm against gross abuses of human rights has been established, but its future enforcement remains uncertain. Lastly, there is the problem of deterring (and compelling) collectively, of convincing targets that coalitions of states are prepared to overcome their differences and follow through on threats. This creates new problems of credibility.[9]

The attempts to establish these various norms came together during the course of the campaign against the regime of Saddam Hussein leading up to the 2003 war. There were few crimes of which this regime had not been guilty in the past, even when Western countries had viewed it with greater tolerance: serial abuse of human rights, persecution of minorities, aggression against neighbours, support for terrorism, support for subversion, plundering of assets, development, production and use of WMD, non-compliance with UN resolutions. Why then was there so much international opposition to the military operation mounted by the USA and UK? Part of this was a reaction to what was perceived to be the potential abuse of military hegemony. There was discomfort with the idea of a world in which states that had earned the disapproval of these two powers could be taken over at will and with ease. From that concern flowed the argument that such operations should be undertaken only with the express authority of the United Nations. While the issue was firmly under the purview of the UN, there was little consensus about how far it could be taken. There was no agreement about the severity or the intractability of the particular issue that prompted the war – that is, the alleged existence, despite numerous resolutions, of WMD activity. The issue therefore became one not of how to deal with Saddam Hussein, but of the checks and balances on American behaviour, and the readiness of Washington to work through international organizations. This was not, however, a clear test of the issue, given the record of UN resolutions covering Iraq. With Afghanistan as well there was plenty of cover in UN resolutions following 9/11, accepting that terrorism by non-state actors could be considered a threat to international peace and security, for American action. Nonetheless, this case showed up the importance of legitimacy in international affairs, and it was highlighted further when the USA sought to draw other states into the policing of post-war Iraq only to find that there were few takers, in part because of the perceived illegitimacy of the occupation.

How far is the United States likely to push in the future? The extension of ideological influence does not depend on armed force. It can result from the activities of multinational corporations, the influence of global media, domestic legislation with extraterritorial impact or conditions attached to funding international bodies and projects. Through these means may come a range of pressures, not necessarily all pointing in one direction, encouraging secularism on the one hand and religious-based objections to abortion on the other, free markets and prohibitions on child labour, and the English language and music. It would be quite unsuitable to back these pressures with force, but in some cases they can seem as threatening as any military intervention, and may even lead to a reaction that dismays a local population as modernity is resisted at all costs. This may not seem the normal menu for discussions of deterrence, but its salience can be high.

After Iraq there was a question of whether the remaining members of the 'axis of evil', North Korea and Iran, or candidate members such as Syria and Libya, would be targeted. On the one hand the effort involved in the reconstruction of Iraq has been salutary for Washington policy-makers; on the other, there is evidence to show that some of the regimes in question recognized that they were caught up in a process that would as likely as not require changes in their domestic practices and foreign policies. Libya, for example, after competing with Iraq for the top spot in Western demonology managed, without a change in leadership, to adjust. This was, in part, as noted above, because of the UN sanctions imposed in connection with the extradition of the likely culprits of the explosion of a bomb on a US aircraft flying above the Scottish town of Lockerbie in 1989. Syria, a radical but secular regime, with a backward economy, rejectionist attitudes towards Israel, a history of support of militant Palestinian groups and occupation of a neighbour (Lebanon), became vulnerable once Saddam Hussein fell. It moved sharply to demonstrate that it was not providing a sanctuary for former Iraqi leaders, to ensure that the United States had no grounds for an early attack. The Iranians also took care, although as the US occupation began to face difficulties in establishing security and maintaining a steady political course within Iraq, they became aware that the Americans might need their help in keeping the Shi'ite majority calm as elements among the Sunni population increased their attacks against the occupying forces. At the same time extremist groups began to see opportunities in Iraq to cause the Americans discomfort and even to compel them to leave. All this indicates the extent to which all political groups, however apparently fanatical in their ideology, adjust to shifting power relationships and act with some thought to the consequences.

The principles that might inform foreign policy do not always point in the same direction. That is the nature of principles and their value in policy debate. It is precisely because they can be weighed against each other that they avoid the rigidity of authoritative rules that must be applied come what may. They are by their nature indeterminate and because the facts of each case will vary they will have varying implications. This is why foreign policies that claim to be based on broad principles inevitably lead to accusations of double standards. Why deal with this awful tyrant when here is another with as much blood on his hands? The answer may lie in what can prudently be done with the resources available, especially if the principles of proportionality are to be respected. It will still be necessary to face the natural cynicism of those who assume that norm-setting is a charade and nothing is done except in self-interest.

While the principles at play in contemporary international affairs do not always reinforce each other, as the debates over both Kosovo and Iraq demonstrated, the weightings are changing. The past commitment to the sovereignty of others, reflected in promises not to interfere in internal affairs, has been systematically qualified with every instance of internal brutality, ensuring that the case for external intervention is made, even if prudential considerations mean that it is not acted upon. Where the oppression is intense, the use of force begins to seem appropriate. So in some cases humanitarian distress may lead to a form of humanitarian pre-emption, as many wish had happened in Rwanda in 1994, when the evidence of tragedy is just too unambiguous and harrowing to allow procrastination. There may also be cases when a state that has harboured and encouraged terrorists finds itself having to take responsibility for their most obnoxious activities. The more such cases are acted upon, the more the message will get through, and others will take the hint. Suggestions that an irritating segment of the population might be expelled or crushed, or that some naive extremists might usefully be helped as they set about subverting a neighbouring rival, start to acquire risks that they previously lacked. Provocative decisions become that much more difficult.

Norm-setting requires a keen understanding of the sources of legitimacy in contemporary international affairs. The authority of the United States acting on its own is inherently limited, and the limits grow when it acts as if norms and international institutions are for others and not for itself. The value of legitimate processes is that they help find ways through those cases when principles are in conflict, or when the enforcement of principles requires that some states accept great risks and costs. To the extent that the possible use of force is part of these processes of norm-setting, then a policy of strategic deterrence can be considered to be in play. It does not follow classical deterrence theory, but it can draw on the old debates. Credibility issues are still raised when exertions have to be made on behalf of third parties, or when the enforcement costs appear high, or when the threats attempt to restrain too much. Communications will have to be constructed with multiple audiences in mind, and the possibilities of misperceptions will require attention. There will be a degree of bargaining, but acceptance of second-best solutions will have to be judged against the precedents that might be created for the future. Success will be judged by good behaviour resulting not from a sharp adjustment in the course of an immediate crisis, but through the internalizing of the norms to the point where they no longer need external reinforcement. Deterrence then will not be the driver of foreign policy but the benign consequences of its underlying consistency and coherence.

NOTES

INTRODUCTION

1 Patrick M. Morgan, *Deterrence Now* (Cambridge: Cambridge University Press, 2003).

CHAPTER 1 THE RISE AND FALL OF DETERRENCE

1 These examples are taken from John Renmaker, *Dr Strangelove and the Hideous Epoch: Deterrence in the Nuclear Age* (Claremont, CA: Regina Books, 2000), p. 145.
2 Jeremy Bentham, *The Rationale of Punishment* (Robert Heward, 1830); derived from manuscripts of Bentham written in the 1770s. ⟨http://www.la.utexas.edu/labyrinth/rp/index.html⟩
3 John Foster Dulles, 'The Evolution of Foreign Policy', Department of State Bulletin, XXX (25 January 1954). Reprinted in Philip Bobbit, Lawrence Freedman and Greg Treverton, eds, *US Nuclear Strategy: A Reader* (London: Macmillan, 1989).
4 Bernard Brodie, ed., *The Absolute Weapon* (New York: Harcourt Brace, 1946), p. 31. I deal with the history of nuclear strategy and deterrence in Lawrence Freedman, *The Evolution of Nuclear Strategy*, 3rd edn (London: Palgrave, 2003).
5 Henry Kissinger, *Diplomacy* (New York: Simon & Schuster, 1994), p. 608.

6   Stanley Hoffman, 'The Acceptability of Military Force', *Force in Modern Societies: Its Place in International Politics*, ed. François Duchene (London: International Institute for Strategic Studies, 1973), p. 6.

7   For an example, see John Lewis Gaddis, *The Long Peace: Inquiries into the History of the Second World War* (New York: Oxford University Press, 1987).

8   Michael Howard, 'Lessons of the Cold War', *Survival*, 36 (Winter 1994–5): 161, 164; see also John Mueller, *Retreat from Doomsday* (New York: Basic Books, 1989); John Lewis Gaddis, Philip H. Gordon, Ernest R. May and Jonathan Rosenberg, *Cold War Statesmen Confront the Bomb: Nuclear Diplomacy Since 1945* (Oxford: Oxford University Press, 1999).

9   Thomas Schelling, *The Strategy of Conflict* (Oxford: Oxford University Press, 1960), p. 193. For a later demonstration of how accidents might have led to escalation, see Scott D. Sagan, *The Limits of Safety: Organizations, Accidents and Nuclear Weapons* (Princeton: Princeton University Press, 1993).

10 McGeorge Bundy, 'The Bishops and the Bomb', *The New York Review* (16 June 1983). For a discussion of 'existentialist' literature, see Lawrence Freedman, 'I Exist; Therefore I Deter', *International Security* (Summer 1988).

11 Robert Jervis, 'Deterrence Theory Revisited', *World Politics*, 31:2 (January 1979): 289–324.

12 Irving Janis, *Victims of Group-think* (Boston: Houghton Mifflin, 1972); Graham Allison, *Essence of Decision: Explaining the Cuban Missile Crisis* (New York: 1971). Second editions of these books came out in 1982 and 1999 respectively. Robert Jervis, *Perception and Misperception in International Politics* (Princeton: Princeton University Press, 1976).

13 Jeffrey D. Berejikian, 'A Cognitive Theory of Deterrence', *Journal of Peace Research*, 39:2 (2002): 165–83, p. 165.

14 Alexander George and Richard Smoke, *Deterrence in American Foreign Policy* (New York: Columbia University Press, 1974).

15 Richard Ned Lebow and Janice Stein, *We All Lost the Cold War* (Princeton: Princeton University Press, 1994).

16 On this see, for example, the work of Keith Payne, *Deterrence in the Second Nuclear Age* (Lexington: University Press of Kentucky, 1996); *The Fallacies of Cold War Deterrence and a New Direction* (Lexington: University Press of Kentucky, 2001).

17   Charles Krauthammer, 'The Obsolescence of Deterrence', *The Weekly Standard* (12 September 2002): 8:13.
18   Colin Gray, *Maintaining Effective Deterrence* (Carlisle, PA: Strategic Studies Institute, US Army War College, August 2003), p. vi.

CHAPTER 2   THE MEANING OF DETERRENCE

1   Lawrence Freedman, ed., *Strategic Coercion: Concepts and Cases* (London: Oxford University Press, 1998).
2   Patrick Morgan, *Deterrence: A Conceptual Analysis* (Beverly Hills, CA: Sage Publications, 1977).
3   In fact, Falstaff's objective was to use deception to give the appearance of having been valorous, and suffer for it, in order to deny the reality of having been deterred. (See Shakespeare, *King Henry IV. Part I*, Act V, sc. 4.)
4   *On Thermonuclear War* (Princeton: Princeton University Press, 1961), pp. 126ff. and 282ff.
5   *Deterrence by Denial and Punishment* (Princeton: Center of International Studies, 1958). See also Snyder's *Deterrence and Defense* (Princeton: Princeton University Press, 1961).
6   John Mearsheimer, *Conventional Deterrence* (Ithaca: Cornell University Press, 1983); Samuel Huntington, 'Conventional Deterrence and Conventional Retaliation', *International Security*, 8:3 (Winter 1983/84): 32–56; Jonathan Shimshoni, *Israel and Conventional Deterrence: Border Warfare from 1953 to 1970* (Ithaca: Cornell University Press, 1988).
7   Steve Walt, 'Rigor or Rigor Mortis, Rational Choice and Security Studies', *International Security*, 23:4 (Spring 1999): 29.
8   Richard J. Harknett, 'The Logic of Conventional Deterrence and the End of the Cold War', *Security Studies*, 4:1 (Autumn 1994): 86–114.
9   Morgan, *Deterrence: A Conceptual Analysis*, pp. 28, 29, 30, 40–3.

CHAPTER 3   DETERRENCE IN PRACTICE

1   See for example Dale Copeland, 'A Realist Critique of the English School', *Review of International Studies*, 29:3 (July 2003): 430–1, who argues that against this test the 'English School' of international relations fails. Against this test,

however, it is not obvious that any school that seeks to say anything interesting can possibly prosper.

2 The analytical work in this area has been dominated by two teams: Richard Ned Lebow/Janice Stein and Paul Huth/Bruce Russett. In 1990 the first team published a critique of the second in 'Deterrence: The Elusive Dependent Variable', *World Politics*, 42:3 (April 1990): 336–69. Huth and Russett replied with 'Testing Deterrence Theory: Rigor Makes a Difference', *World Politics*, 42:4 (April 1990): 466–501. Richard Ned Lebow and Janice Gross Stein, *When Does Deterrence Succeed and How Do We Know?* (Ottawa: Canadian Institute for International Peace and Security, February 1990). Paul Huth, *Extended Deterrence and the Prevention of War* (New Haven: Yale University Press, 1988), p. 13.

3 B. Alexander George, 'Case Studies and Theory Development: The Method of Structured, Focused Comparison', in P. G. Lauren, ed., *Diplomacy: New Approaches in History, Theory, and Policy* (New York: Free Press, 1979), pp. 43–68.

4 Christopher Achen and Duncan Snidal, 'Rational Deterrence Theory and Comparative Case Studies', *World Politics*, 41 (January 1989): 143–69. The most thorough attempt to develop a data set on deterrence, covering 1895 to 1985, can be found in Vesna Danilovic, *When the Stakes are High: Deterrence and Conflict among Great Powers* (Ann Arbor: University of Michigan Press, 2002).

5 Lebow and Stein, 'Deterrence', pp. 343–4. The conceptual source for this very particular type of deterrence is discussed in the next chapter. Part of the difficulty in comparing cases of this nature is that they would not have been discussed in those terms in their own time but would have been addressed through the language of alliance and security guarantees.

6 More recent inductive theorists have sought to understand deterrence less in terms of one-off episodes and more as a series of encounters within a structured conflict. See Elli Lieberman, 'The Rational Deterrence Theory Debate: Is the Dependent Variable Elusive?', *Security Studies*, 3:3 (Spring 1994): 389–90; Paul Huth and Bruce Russett, 'General Deterrence Between Enduring Rivals: Testing Three Competing Models', *American Political Science Review*, 87:1 (March 1993). Lebow and Stein, 'Deterrence', p. 342.

7   Janice Gross Stein, 'Deterrence and Learning in an Enduring Rivalry', *Security Studies*, 6:1 (Autumn 1996): 104–52.

8   Alexander George and Richard Smoke, *Deterrence in American Foreign Policy* (New York: Columbia University Press, 1974). Lebow and Stein, 'Deterrence', pp. 590–1.

9   Robert Jervis, 'Deterrence Theory Revisited', *World Politics*, 31:2 (January 1979): 314–15. Danilovic, *When the Stakes are High*, argues that the deterrent threats by major powers gain 'inherent credibility' when applied in support of protégés in situations in which they have high regional stakes.

10 Alexander L. George and William E. Simons, eds, *The Limits of Coercive Diplomacy* (Boulder: Westview, 1994).

11 Keith Payne, *The Fallacies of Cold War Deterrence and a New Direction* (Lexington: University Press of Kentucky, 2001), pp. 7–15.

12 Patrick Morgan, 'Saving Face for the Sake of Deterrence', in Robert Jervis, Richard Ned Lebow and Janice Gross Stein, *Psychology and Deterrence* (Baltimore: Johns Hopkins University Press, 1985), p. 136.

13 Ibid., p. 149.

14 Tom Schelling, *Arms and Influence* (New Haven: Yale University Press, 1996), p. 194.

15 On this, see Stephen Maxwell, *Rationality in Deterrence*, Adelphi Paper No. 50 (London: IISS, 1968), pp. 18–19.

16 'Counterforce and Alliance: The Ultimate Connection', *International Security*, 6:4 (1982): 28, cited in Morgan, 'Saving Face', p. 135.

17 Huth, *Extended Deterrence*.

18 Jonathan Mercer, *Reputation and International Politics* (Ithaca: Cornell University Press, 1996), pp. 6, 9, 228. As an example of the stress on reputation in deterrence theory see Roger Powell, *Nuclear Deterrence Theory: The Search for Credibility* (Cambridge: Cambridge University Press, 1990).

19 Critiques of Mercer by Dale C. Copeland and Paul Huth, with a reply by Mercer, can be found in *Security Studies*, 7:1 (August 1997).

20 Ted Hopf, *Peripheral Visions: Deterrence Theory and American Foreign Policy in the Third World, 1965–1990* (Ann Arbor: University of Michigan Press, 1994), pp. 233, 241.

21 Richard Ned Lebow, 'Deterrence and Reassurance: Lessons from the Cold War', *Global Dialogue* (Autumn 2001): 128.

See also Janice Stein, 'Deterrence and Reassurance', in Philip Tetlock et al. eds., *Behavior Society and Nuclear War*, vol. 2 (New York: Oxford University Press, 1991).

22   Stephen R. Rock, *Appeasement in International Politics* (Lexington: University Press of Kentucky, 2000).

23   Michael D. Young and Mark Schafer, 'Is There Method in Our Madness? Ways of Assessing Cognition in International Relations', *Mershon International Studies Review* (1998): 42, 63–96.

24   Robert Jervis, 'Deterrence and Perception', in Steve Miller, ed., *Strategy and Nuclear Deterrence* (Princeton: Princeton University Press, 1984), p. 58.

25   Achen and Snidal, 'Rational Deterrence Theory', p. 157.

CHAPTER 4 NORMS AND CRIMINALITY

1   Daniel S. Nagin and Greg Pogarsky, 'Integrating Celerity, Impulsivity, and Extralegal Sanction Threats into a Model of General Deterrence: Theory and Evidence', *Criminology*, 39:4 (November 2001): 865–92.

2   Roger Hood notes that the numbers favouring the death penalty because of its deterrent effect is remarkably low. See his *The Death Penalty: A Worldwide Perspective*, 3rd edn (London: Oxford University Press, 2002), p. 241. Retributive reasons accounted for over half of an American sample in a February 2001 poll, with only 10 per cent endorsing the penalty for deterrence purposes. Hood's book provides an excellent survey of the evidence on this issue.

3   Isaac Ehrlich, 1975 'The Deterrent Effect of Capital Punishment: A Question of Life and Death', *American Economic Review*, 65 (1975): 397–417; Stephen K. Layson, 'Homicide and Deterrence: A Reexamination of the United States Time-Series Evidence', *Southern Economic Journal*, 52 (1985): 68–89.

4   Alfred Blumstein, Jacqueline Cohen and Daniel Nagin, eds, *Deterrence and Incapacitation: Estimating the Effects of Criminal Sanctions on Crime Rates* (Washington, DC: National Academy of Sciences).

5   Michael L. Radelet and Ronald L. Akers, *Deterrence and the Death Penalty: The Views of the Experts*, ⟨http://sun.soci.niu.edu/~critcrim/dp/dppapers/mike.deterrence⟩

6   Andrew von Hirsch, Anthony E. Bottoms, Elizabeth Burney and P.-O. Wikstrom, *Criminal Deterrence and Sentence Severity: An Analysis of Recent Research* (Oxford: Hart Publishing, 1999).

7   Kirk Williams and Richard Hawkins, 'Perceptual Research on General Deterrence: A Critical Overview', *Law and Society Review*, 20 (1986): 545–72. Daniel Nagin has been particularly active in pursuing this line of inquiry. See his 'Criminal Deterrence Research at the Outset of the Twenty-first Century', in M. Tonry, ed., *Crime and Justice: A Review of Research*, vol. 23 (Chicago: University of Chicago Press, 1998).

8   The key text is Hedley Bull, *The Anarchical Society* (London: Macmillan, 1977).

9   Jeffrey T. Checkel, 'The Constructivist Turn in International Relations Theory', *World Politics*, 50:2 (1998): 324–48; Theo Farrell, 'Constructivist Security Studies: Portrait of a Research Program', *International Studies Review*, 4:1 (Spring 2002); Ted Hopf, 'The Promise of Constructivism in International Relations Theory', *International Security*, 23 (1998): 171–200; Alexander Wendt, *Social Theory of International Politics* (Cambridge: Cambridge University Press, 1999).

10   'Introduction', in Peter J. Katzenstein, ed., *The Culture of National Security: Norms and Identity in World Politics* (New York: Columbia University Press, 1996), p. 5.

11   Thomas Schelling, 'The Legacy of Hiroshima: A Half-Century Without Nuclear War', *The Key Reporter*, the quarterly publication of the Phi Beta Kappa Society, 65:3 (Spring 2000). ⟨http://www.puaf.umd.edu/IPPP/Summer00/legacy_of_hiroshima.htm⟩

12   Richard Price and Nina Tannenwald, 'Norms and Deterrence: The Nuclear Weapons Taboo', in Peter J. Katzenstein, ed., *The Culture of National Security: Norms and Identity in World Politics* (New York: Columbia University Press, 1996), pp. 114–53; Richard Price, *The Chemical Weapons Taboo* (Ithaca, NY: Cornell University Press, 1997); Nina Tannenwald, 'The Nuclear Taboo: The United States and the Normative Basis of Nuclear Non-Use', *International Organization*, 53:3 (Summer 1999): 433–68.

13   Michael C. Desch, 'Culture Clash: Assessing the Importance of Ideas in Security Studies', *International Security*, 23 (Summer 1998): 1.

14   Philip Jenkins, *Images of Terror: What We Can and Can't Know About Terrorism* (New York: Walter de Gruyter, 2003).

15   Ward Thomas, 'Norms and Security: The Case of International Assassination', *International Security*, 25:1 (2000): 121.

16   Paul Kowert and Jeffrey Legro, 'Norms, Identity, and Their Limits', in Peter J. Katzenstein, ed., *The Culture of National Security: Norms and Identity in World Politics* (New York: Columbia University Press, 1996), pp. 485–6, n. 81.

17   Lee Ann Fujii, 'The Diffusion of a Genocidal Norm in Rwanda'. Paper prepared for the Annual Convention of the International Studies Association, New Orleans, LA, 24–27 March 2002. ⟨http://www.isanet.org/noarchive/rwanda.html⟩

18   Robert Axelrod, 'An Evolutionary Approach to Norms', *American Political Science Review*, 80:4 (December 1986): 1095–111; Ann Florini, 'The Evolution of International Norms', *International Studies Quarterly*, 40 (1996): 363–89.

19   Fujii, 'The Diffusion of a Genocidal Norm in Rwanda', pp. 4–5.

20   I take this to be reasonably self-evident. Christopher Gelpi develops the point through political science methodology in 'Crime and Punishment: The Role of Norms in Crisis Bargaining', *The American Political Science Review*, 91:2 (June 1997), pp. 339–60.

CHAPTER 6 FROM DETERRENCE TO PRE-EMPTION

1   Jack Levy, 'Declining Power and the Preventive Motivation for War', *World Politics*, 40:1 (October 1987), distinguishes between the two concepts on the basis of time.

2   M. Elaine Bunn, *Preemptive Action: When, How, and to What effect?*, Strategic Forum, No. 200, National Defense University, July 2003, p. 8.

3   A. Parsons, *From Cold War to Hot Peace: UN Interventions 1947–1994* (London: Michael Joseph, 1995), pp. 44, 45, 52, 53–4.

4   *Further Report of the Secretary-General on the Implementation of Security Council Resolution 598 (1987)* (New York: United Nations, 1991).

5   Address to National Defence University, 15 January 1986. Cited in Michael Byers, 'Preemptive Self-defense: Changing

the Rules to Accommodate the Exception', *Ethics and International Affairs*, 16 (2003).

6   Brad Roberts, 'NBC-Armed Rogues: Is There a Moral Case for Preemption?' in Elliott Abrams, ed., *Close Calls: Intervention, Terrorism, Missile Defense, and 'Just War' Today* (Ethics and Public Policy Center, 2002). In the late 1980s, the USA had made similar warnings about the Libyan chemical facility at Ratba, which the Libyan leader, Colonel Gaddafi, later conveniently reported to have burnt down.

7   The National Security Strategy paper is found on ⟨www.whitehouse.gov/nsc⟩

8   Ibid.

9   Bunn, *Preemptive Action*, p. 6.

10   Condoleezza Rice, speech to the Manhattan Institute, 1 October 2002.

11   Condoleezza Rice, 'Campaign 2000: Promoting the National Interest', *Foreign Affairs* (January/February 2000).

12   For a fascinating analysis of this language, see Raymond Tanter, *Classifying Evil: Bush Administration Rhetoric and Policy Toward Rogue Regimes*, Research Memorandum 44 (Washington Institute for Near East Policy, 2003).

13   *New York Times*, 1 February 2003. Cited in Robert Jervis, 'The Bush Doctrine: Fear, Opportunity, and Expansion', *Political Science Quarterly*, 118 (Fall 2003).

14   Kenneth Pollack, 'Containment, Deterrence, Preemption', *Foreign Affairs* (March/April 2002).

15   Michael Quinlan, 'War on Iraq: A Blunder and a Crime', *Financial Times*, 6 August 2002.

16   Thomas L. Friedman, 'Deterrence at Last', *New York Times*, 13 February 2002.

17   Thomas L. Friedman, 'The Iraq Debate is Upside Down', *International Herald Tribune*, 19 September 2002.

18   Michael Dobbs, 'N. Korea Tests Bush's Policy of Preemption Strategy Seems to Target Weaker Nations', *Washington Post*, 6 January 2003, p. A0; Mike Allen and Barton Gellman, 'Preemptive Strikes Part of US Strategic Doctrine: "All Options" Open for Countering Unconventional Arms', *Washington Post*, 11 December 2002.

19   Dan Reiter, 'Exploding the Powder Keg Myth: Preemptive Wars Almost Never Happen', *International Security*, 20 (Fall 1995): 5–34.

20   Ibid., p. 33.
21   Bunn, *Preemptive Action*, p. 4.
22   Michael E. O'Hanlon, Susan E. Rice and James B. Steinberg, *The New National Security Strategy and Preemption* (Washington, DC: Brookings Institution Policy Brief, 2002; Policy Brief #113, December 2002).
23   Jack Snyder, 'Imperial Temptations', *The National Interest* (Spring 2003).
24   National Security Strategy, p. 28.
25   Michael R. Gordon, 'How Bush Preemptive Doctrine was Born', *International Herald Tribune*, 27 January 2003.
26   Michael Glennon, 'Military Action Against Terrorists Under International Law: The Fog of Law: Self-Defense, Inherence, and Incoherence in Article 51 of the United Nations Charter', *Harvard Journal of Law and Public Policy*, 539 (2002). See also Anthony Clark Arend, 'International Law and the Preemptive Use of Military Force', *The Washington Quarterly*, 26:2 (Spring 2003): 89–103.
27   Charles Kegley and Gregory A. Raymond, 'Preventive War and Permissive Normative Order', *International Studies Perspectives*, 4:4 (November 2003): 391.

CHAPTER 7 STRATEGIC COERCION

1   Thomas Schelling, *Arms and Influence* (New Haven, CT: Yale University Press, 1966).
2   Alexander L. George and William E. Simons, eds, *The Limits of Coercive Diplomacy* (Boulder, CO: Westview, 1994). A second edition was published in 1994, reflecting the belief in the relevance of changed circumstances.
3   Lawrence Freedman, ed., *Strategic Coercion: Concepts and Cases* (London: Oxford University Press, 1998).
4   Schelling, *Arms and Influence*, pp. 69, 73, 75, 175.
5   George and Simons, *The Limits of Coercive Diplomacy*, p. 2.
6   Ibid, p. 293.

CHAPTER 8 THE FUTURE OF DETERRENCE

1   Colin Gray, *Maintaining Effective Deterrence* (Carlisle, PA: Strategic Studies Institute, US Army War College, August 2003), pp. 18, 30.

2   Patrick M. Morgan, *Deterrence Now* (Cambridge: Cambridge University Press, 2003), pp. 285–6. This conclusion survives two recent books which, in their different ways, have sought to produce rigorous analyses of deterrence: Frank Zagare and D. Marc Kilgour, *Perfect Deterrence* (Cambridge: Cambridge University Press, 2000) which adopts a game theoretic approach, and the inductive methodology of Vesna Danilovic, *When the Stakes are High* (Ann Arbor: University of Michigan Press, 2002).

3   Robert Ross, 'Navigating the Taiwan Strait: Deterrence, Escalation, and US–China Relations', *International Security*, 27 (Fall 2002): 48–85.

4   Kenneth Waltz, *The Spread of Nuclear Weapons: More May Be Better*, Adelphi Paper 171 (London: IISS, 1981). The issue is debated with Scott Sagan in *The Spread of Nuclear Weapons: A Debate* (New York: Norton, 1995). For a recent critique, see Richard L. Russell, 'The Nuclear Peace Fallacy: How Deterrence Can Fail', *Journal of Strategic Studies*, 26:1 (March 2003): 136–55.

5   For an optimistic view, see Devin T. Hagerty, 'Nuclear Deterrence in South Asia: The 1990 Indo-Pakistani Crisis', *International Security*, 20:3 (Winter 1995).

6   Daniel Benjamin and Steven Simon, 'The Next Debate: Al Qaeda Link', *New York Times*, 20 July 2003.

7   These are developed in Neil J. Smelser and Faith Mitchell, eds, *Discouraging Terrorism: Some Implications of 9/11*, Panel on Understanding Terrorists in Order to Deter Terrorism, Center for Social and Economic Studies, Division of Behavioral and Social Sciences, National Research Council of the National Academies (Washington, DC: The National Academies Press, 2002).

8   Robert Pape, 'The Strategic Logic of Suicide Terrorism', *American Political Science Review*, 97:3 (August 2003).

9   This issue is fully explored in Morgan, *Deterrence Now*, ch. 6.

INDEX

general, 40–2, 45–6, 65, 67,
    75
immediate, 40–2, 45–6, 65,
    75
internalized, 31–2, 46, 59,
    65
narrow, 32–4
through denial, 36–40, 60
through punishment, 36–40,
    60–7, 72, 110, 124
Deterrence (film), 25
Dr Strangelove (film), 25
Dulles, John Foster, 8–9, 12, 70

Egypt, 90
Ehrlich, Isaac, 62
Eisenhower, President Dwight
    Administration of, 40, 70, 87
'English School', 68, 133
escalation, 34, 37, 76, 78

Fail-safe (film), 25
Falklands War, 118
Falstaff, 30
'first wave' theory, 21
First World War, 32, 71, 103
France, 2, 82, 91, 94, 97, 125
Friedman, Thomas, 100–1

George, Alexander, 23, 44,
    46–7, 109–11
Georgia, 103
Germany, 2, 33
Gibbs, Jack, 62
Glennon, Michael, 107–8
Gulf War, 70, 93, 96–7, 101,
    114–15

Harknett, Richard, 39
Hitler, Adolf, 57
Hopf, Ted, 55–6

Howard, John, 94
Huth, Paul, 43, 53
Huntington, Samuel, 38
Hussein, Saddam, 2, 91,
    96–101, 104, 115, 118,
    121, 126–8

imperialism, 77
India, 48, 103, 120
Indonesia, 123
Iran, 91–2, 96, 98–9, 113, 121,
    128
Iran–Iraq war, 91–2, 113
Iraq, 25, 70, 90–1, 114–15,
    125
    2003 war, 2–4, 96–102,
    104–5, 108, 121, 123,
    126–9
Israel, 38, 90–1, 103, 112,
    128

Japan, 33, 36, 48, 87, 94,
    102
Jervis, Robert, 21–2, 46, 58
Jordan, 90

Kahn, Herman, 35
Kennedy, John, 18, 88
Kissinger, Henry, 11
Korean War, 33, 103
Kosovo War, 82, 106–7, 114,
    125, 129
Kuwait, 25, 70, 81, 96,
    114–15, 121

Laden, Osama bin, 98, 115,
    123
Lebanon, 128
Lebow, Richard Ned, 23, 43,
    45–6, 56
Libya, 92–3, 121, 128, 138